# Living with Your Passions

*A Christian's Guide to Sexual Purity*

D1714146

Erwin W. Lutzer

Moody Church Media
Chicago

*Cover by Bryan Butler*

**LIVING WITH YOUR PASSIONS**
Copyright © 2024 by Erwin W. Lutzer
Published by Moody Church Media
Chicago, Illinois 60614
www.moodymedia.org

ISBN: 9798321320242

# CONTENTS

ERWIN W. LUTZER

## CHAPTER ONE

# THE BATTLE WITH PASSIONS

"I got saved six months ago, but nobody told my glands!" Most of us identify with this 18-year-old, in a conflict as old as the human race: the struggle of sexual feelings against the restraints of conscience and the teachings of the Bible. Our passions cry *yes* when our better moral judgment cries *no!*

The teachings of the New Testament warn against sexual promiscuity (1 Corinthians 6:18). Jesus taught that everyone who looks at another with lust has already committed adultery inwardly (Matthew 5:28). This precept, along with others Jesus taught, conflict with the strong sexual desires tantalizing so many of us. How can we obey God's teachings when our sexual urges feel so right, so proper, so beautiful?

More than one Christian, overcome by sexual temptation, has bought a pornographic magazine or has clicked through a pornographic website. One man told me that when his lust was satisfied, he was so disgusted with himself that he burned the magazine in the bathroom sink or blocked the website on his computer or phone. Yet an hour later, he was back sifting through the ashes or searching for another website, hoping to find some erotic pictures which had escaped his feeble attempt to destroy the evidence! Such is the dilemma of sexual misconduct: Its victims alternate between exhilaration and disgust.

How do we handle the conflict? Some surrender to the pressures of their sexual appetite. They choose the steep and attractive path of moral laxity. Believing they are free to stop at any point along the decline, they take that first step. If there are no immediate negative consequences, they continue, not knowing that well-concealed pitfalls await them along the way.

It may begin with pornography, a passionate kiss, or experiencing the exhilaration of sexual attraction toward someone other than their spouse. How the first step is taken makes little difference. The point is that in taking this first step downward, these people are no longer taking advantage of God's restraints. They are in enemy territory, though they may not know it at this point. Perhaps years will pass before they realize that God's restrictions were for their own good. Meanwhile, the scenery on the far side of the hill is too captivating; there's no time to contemplate the possible effects of their actions.

## ON THE SLIPPERY SLOPE

Among those who have wandered off on their own and fallen down the slippery slope can be sorted into at least two distinct groups. In one group are those who are enjoying themselves and have no thought of returning to solid ground. Christians or not, they've decided they know better than God; they will chart their own course without the benefit of the warning signs they've chosen to ignore. They naively believe they can control the consequences of their actions—they are sure they've found a better way. Even when they suspect they're wrong, they stubbornly refuse to admit it. Better to live with emptiness and guilt; better to be spiritually bankrupt than to acknowledge a need for help and humbly return to God for forgiveness and moral direction.

Someone has said the world is like a ship about to sink in the deepest ocean. When the captain knows the ship is sinking, he says to the passengers: "Those of you who are in second class may pass to first class without paying. Drink all the whiskey you want—everything is free. If you want to break the lamps or smash the furniture, do it!" The passengers are impressed with the broadmindedness of their captain. Why wouldn't they obey him? They've got all the freedom they want—anything they desire. On a sinking ship, anything is possible.

Many today are enjoying a sensual life without admitting

their ship is on the way down. Preoccupation with pleasure has long since deadened their spiritual perception. Like the children of Lot, they heed warnings with scorn and take them as jokes (Genesis 19:14). But their ship is sinking and God will write the final chapter of their lives. Their eventual judgment is inevitable.

In the other group are those who have wandered into moral quicksand but would like to return to the gracious forgiveness and deliverance God can give them. They have fallen; they've become soiled, and their consciences are constant reminders of their disobedience. A man has seduced another man's wife; a boy has been introduced to homosexuality by a friend; a beautiful sixteen-year-old must admit to her parents that she is pregnant; and a young woman carries with her the secret that she had an abortion.

What all of these people have in common is a desire for a new beginning. They'd like to put their past behind them. They wish they had trusted God rather than their own judgment, but they don't know how to get back to where they began. They've tried to stand up—God knows they have—but they've fallen again and again. They're almost ready to give up. They need to be encouraged and to realize they can be freed from repeated failures. The consequences of their actions may never change, but they *can* change. More accurately, God can change them!

## OBEYING THE WARNING SIGNALS

Others have heeded the counsel of Scripture, and intend to live within the boundaries of God's will. They don't commit adultery, watch sensual movies, or abuse their authority for sexual favors. Fortunately, they have not had to endure the shame and guilt associated with sexual misconduct. If they don't know it already, someday they'll discover they have taken the best path.

However, among them are those who feel frustrated and cheated. They envy those of the younger generation who have experienced the pleasure of sexual promiscuity. At times, they wish they could throw caution to the wind. If they ever got the big city where no one knows them, they might indulge in "adult" entertainment, go clubbing, and make up for what they've been missing. Perhaps they feel the church, or for that matter God, has not been fair with them. They've missed some thrills.

For now, however, perhaps because of fear, they remain within the bounds of an acceptable moral code. Yet they stand on tiptoe, trying to satisfy their curiosity and wondering what it's like on the other side. They have yet to learn that God has not cheated them; they need not envy the wicked, and most importantly, that it is possible to be satisfied within God's prescribed limits. For those who are single, this means sexual abstinence. They will be denied the pleasures of sexual intimacy. They will learn that even this—painful though it may be for some—is better than the attractive and grossly overrated alternatives. Those who are married must also learn the same lesson, for diverse sexual attractions come to all. Marriage is not a guarantee that sexual desires will be satisfied. Though chastity for the unmarried and fidelity for the married are not popular, such commitments are not only right, they are best. Many believe this in their heads, but not in their hearts.

Others, probably more than we might suspect, live chaste lives and are satisfied. Of course they experience temptations—even powerful temptations—but they are convinced that God has their best interests in mind. They have chosen to follow obediently and are not flirting with forbidden pleasures. For them, the satisfaction of walking with God and having a clear conscience is ample reward for their obedience.

Then there are people who, in the past, have slipped and fallen, but they have accepted God's forgiveness. Paul wrote to the Corinthians: "Or do you not know that the unrighteous will not inherit the kingdom of God? Do not be deceived: neither the sexually immoral, nor idolaters, nor adulterers, nor men who practice homosexuality, nor thieves, nor the greedy, nor drunkards, nor revilers, nor swindlers will inherit the kingdom of God" (1 Corinthians 6:9–10). Yet Paul continues: *"And such were some of you. But you were washed, you were sanctified, you were justified in the name of the Lord Jesus Christ* and by the Spirit of our God" (6:11, italics added). Here is ample proof that God can deliver us from all kinds of sexual misconduct. Habits of the past can be broken and new patterns established. If not, Christ's power must be seriously questioned. Thousands of Christians have been freed from the tyranny of their passions. The battle never subsides; the temptation will always be there regardless of how long we have walked with God. Yet we read, "And those who belong to Christ Jesus have crucified the flesh with its passions and desires" (Galatians 5:24). These promises provide an adequate basis for bringing our passions under the control of the Holy Spirit.

## WHY THIS BOOK?

For years I debated whether to write this book. First, it involves some risks. A friend who teaches marriage seminars said that whatever topic he dealt with on Sunday, he struggled with the next week. Satan, the enemy of our souls, would like to destroy us in areas where we are trying to help God's people. I'm not immune from sexual temptation. Paul warned, "Therefore let anyone who thinks that he stands take heed lest he fall" (1 Corinthians 10:12). The apostle was deeply concerned about the possibility of stumbling as he ran the course of life. In stressing the need for self-control he wrote, "But I discipline my body and keep it under control, lest after preaching to others I myself should be disqualified" (1 Corinthians 9:27). Only the dead are beyond the possibility of sexual misconduct.

Second, I do not claim to be an expert in counseling those who battle with passions. I've lived long enough to realize there is no formula for victory. We cannot expect to have all emotional and sexual problems resolved by reading a book. We are involved in a battle, and that means we must be constantly alert for new strategies both in defense and offense. Superficial guidelines for victory only cause further discouragement, which then leads to unbelief and the hopeless feeling, "That's the way I am...there's no hope for me." The purpose of this book is to map out a general battle strategy to help keep us from acting on our temptations and sinful desires, which will enslave us to our passions.

Third, I have chosen to write this book because I've become thoroughly convinced that the Bible's teaching on sex is for our own good. We all know that sensual pleasure makes incredibly attractive promises. Our passions cry for spontaneous and uninhibited expression, without a hint of any possible negative side effects. In a moment of sexual ecstasy, who cares about what the church or even God has to say! But when the dust settles and all the results are in, when the guilt and shame have been experienced, when the consequences in this life and in the life to come have been thoughtfully calculated, God's way will prove to be the wisest and the best. The question is whether we have the faith to act on this premise without thinking, as Eve did, that we've got to "try it for ourselves."

Finally, I believe that deliverance from sexual misconduct is possible. Oswald Chambers wrote, "If Jesus Christ cannot deliver from sin, if He cannot adjust us perfectly to God as He says He can, if He cannot fill us with the Holy Ghost until there is nothing that can ever appeal again in sin or the world or the flesh, then He has misled us."[1] He's not talking about becoming sinless. He is saying that if Christ cannot deliver us, He has deceived us. Deliverance is possible. I've known people who were freed from promiscuity, pornography, and homosexuality.

Christ may allow our passions to dominate us, at least for a time. He wants to teach us to recognize our weaknesses and our unbelievable penchant for self-justification and rationalization. In the end, however, we can prove Him to be the deliverer He claims to be.

How serious are we in letting God give us self-control over our passions? Like Gideon, we've got to separate the casual soldier from the committed one. So here's the test: Begin by memorizing Colossians 3:1–11 (If then you have been raised with Christ, seek the things that are above...) and don't be satisfied until you know the passage so well you needn't even think about the mechanics. Then you can

concentrate on its meaning. Jesus said, "If you abide in my word, you are truly my disciples, and you will know the truth, and the truth will set you free" (John 8:31–32).

Ready for the challenge?

## STUDY AND APPLICATION

1. What factors in our society and/or culture have contributed to the widespread feeling that sex should be enjoyed apart from commitment and responsibility?

2. John taught that the unsaved walk in darkness, whereas believers should walk in light. What do you think he means by this contrast (1 John 1:5–10).

3. List all the characteristics of the world mentioned in 1 John 2:15–17. Contrast this with the advantages of loving the Father (John 14:23; 15:8–11, etc.).

4. Studies have shown that the viewing habits of Christians and non-Christians are about the same. Discuss the implications of this statement in light of Colossians 3:1–3.

5. In what ways might we subtly imply that Christ is not able to deliver us from the power of sin? In what ways can we correct this misapprehension?

CHAPTER TWO

# THE CONSEQUENCES OF SEXUAL SIN

I begin with David. Not merely because his sin with Bathsheba is already well known. Nor because his story is given so many chapters in the Bible. Nor because his sin is unusual. I begin with David simply because *he's the last man we would expect to find in such a mess!*

After all, David was

- a hero who killed Goliath with a single stone;
- a poet who gave us most of the Psalms;
- a mystic who passionately sought God;
- a king chosen by God and described by the Lord as "a man after My own heart."

Yet it was *that* David who committed adultery then ordered a man be killed to cover it up. Responding to his impulses rather than wisdom, he brought shame and disgrace to himself, his family, and his kingdom.

You've heard the story: The king was taking a late afternoon nap on the flat roof of his palace. When he awoke, he walked around and "was walking on the roof of the king's house, that he saw from the roof a woman bathing; and the woman was very beautiful" (2 Samuel 11:2).

The longer David gazed at her, the more his sexual desires were aroused. His blood ran hot as his eyes were riveted on her shapely body. He watched her in the glow of the setting sun.

There's a world of meaning in the simple phrase "he saw." David's eyes focused on the beautiful naked body. Unfortunately, at that moment, that is *all* David saw. What David did not see is most revealing. He *did not* consider the consequences—the untimely demise of his four sons who would die because of what he was contemplating in his heart. He *did not* anticipate the guilt, the shame, the murder of a man, or the eventual loss of his kingdom. Those concerns were far from his mind at that instant. Tomorrow didn't matter. Maybe he'd even get by with it and nobody would know. Besides, if he didn't invite Bathsheba over for the evening, he'd always wonder what she was *really* like; he'd regret that he didn't take the tantalizing opportunity of enjoying her sexual prowess. He fantasized about conquering a woman he'd never met. What is more, he believed he could make her feel like a woman—fully satisfied.

Let's analyze what happened. There on the rooftop, David made the decision to invite Bathsheba to his palace.

If he was going to reject the temptation, he should have done it then. Perhaps David thought, *I can enjoy this woman vicariously for a time and choose later whether I invite her to my bedroom.* Perhaps yes, perhaps no.

The time to choose against sexual sin is the moment the temptation arises. If we entertain lust, rejecting our passion becomes increasingly difficult. The correct response never becomes easier; every passing moment makes choosing sin more likely. For example, those who view pornography have already made a decision to commit mental adultery; consequently, the decision to commit the act of adultery comes quite easily. Only the *with whom* and the *when* remain undecided.

## YIELDING TO PLEASURE

When David took a long look at Bathsheba, he was cutting the anchor and setting out on a river whose speed and size was rapidly increasing. Returning to shore would become more difficult by the moment. David wasn't thinking about how and when he would return. He enjoyed the sensation of being swept along by the euphoria he felt in his body. He yielded to the pleasure of the moment. He forgot the dangerous rapids ahead.

The next step was predictable. David *sent* messengers to invite her into the palace. I wonder what he said to his servants. Maybe he made an offhand remark about his desire to become better acquainted with his neighbors and wondered who lived two doors down from the palace. Or perhaps after finding out she was the wife of Uriah, one of his mighty men, he used the ruse of wanting to better understand the problems of wives whose husbands were at war. Whatever the excuse, it worked.

The third action was that he "*took* her...and he lay with her" (2 Samuel 11:4, italics added). We don't know to what extent Bathsheba cooperated with David. Did she give in because of the prestige of being in bed with the king? Did she have genuine affection for David? Did she still love her husband, Uriah? Did she feel forced to come as the king's subject? We'll never know.

We also don't know whether David thought about the possibility of her becoming pregnant. Maybe she told him this was her "safe" time of the month, or perhaps she thought she wasn't able to have children. Most likely they didn't think long on these matters—their passions had to be satisfied regardless of the consequences. Whatever the outcome, it could be handled later. Only the present had meaning.

What if Bathsheba had not become pregnant? Perhaps the affair would not have been discovered, Uriah would not have been killed, and David's kingdom would have remained intact. But can we be sure? If we really understand sin, we know we can't escape the judgment of God—even if our actions are unknown to others. We'll discover that sin has enough hidden consequences of its own, apart from public shame. Besides, we can't be sure David's liaison would have remained a secret. What if Bathsheba, overcome with guilt, would have told her husband? Or perhaps she would have used her secret to bribe the king. Possibly the servants who were sent to get her already suspected what happened.

What we *do* know is that she became pregnant and told David the news.

## THE COVER-UP

The king then had to face the fact that this casual affair wasn't as casual as he had imagined. A relationship that began between "two consenting adults" suddenly involved a third person; a baby was on the way. Uriah was also involved, for it was his wife who had secretly betrayed him. David decided he'd have to get Uriah to think the child was his. The king had been checkmated. He lost the first game, but he was determined not to lose the tournament.

Enter *Plan A.* David asked that Uriah be brought to Jerusalem under the pretense of informing the king about the state of the battle in Rabbah. Were they winning or losing? The king would ask him. Then he would send Uriah home, hoping he would make love to his beautiful wife. David would see that a gift accompanied the warrior, hoping it would foster a romantic spirit that would lead the couple into the bedroom.

But Uriah didn't play David's game. We don't know what suspicions he might have had. Did Uriah wonder, "Why all this attention and these special privileges?" He told David he would not go home because he'd feel guilty if he enjoyed his wife when his comrades were fighting under difficult conditions. He stoutly refused the king's offer.

By then David was desperate. He must get Uriah home to make sure the sin would not become known. After all, this was best for the royal family and the entire kingdom.

And so *Plan B* emerged. The king asked Uriah to stay another day so that the two men could eat together. David got him drunk, hoping Uriah would go home in the evening, but the loyal servant stayed with David's servants and did not visit Bathsheba.

If Uriah had gone home and made love to his wife, would David actually have been cleared? Bathsheba would have been forced into both living and telling a lie, of pretending the baby belonged to her husband and lying about the "premature" birth. The child would be a constant reminder of the painful secret that had to be guarded with multiple deceptions.

And David would have to live with the guilt of knowing he was the father of a child who may later discover his true identity. The king would have to carry this secret in his heart, knowing his action had grave consequences in the life of the child. He would also have to live with the fear that Bathsheba might tell Uriah. What if her guilt was too great to bear? Then there was the king's relationship with his wives—what effect would their husband's sexual affair have on them?

But let's return to the story.

David moved to *Plan C.* This was his trump card. He was going to have Uriah killed in battle so Bathsheba could become his wife. He gave Uriah a letter to take to Joab, his military commander. It read in part, "Set Uriah in the forefront of the hardest fighting, and then draw back from him, that he may be struck down, and die" (2 Samuel 11:15).

Why would a good man become a murderer? Why would a good man kill a friend so loyal that he could be trusted to take a letter to his commander without opening it? *Shame causes us to manipulate the consequences of sin.* Beginning with Adam and Eve, mankind has been obsessed with covering sin. The human mind is capable of rationalizing any action the heart craves. We will pay any price to make ourselves look good. David would have been better off if he had admitted his sin outright, despite the humiliation and embarrassment. Instead, he added to his sin, and God's judgment increased proportionately.

Joab obeyed the king's orders and a messenger returned to tell David that Uriah had been killed. David simply replied, "Thus shall you say to Joab, 'Do not let this matter displease you, for the sword devours now one and now another'" (2 Samuel 11:25). Matter-of-factly, David said, "Well, that's life—you win some and you lose some!"

How is the cover-up working? Bathsheba knew, as did Joab and, most likely, the servants. Others would at least suspect when the baby arrived. David knew, and as he later confessed, his sin was "ever before him" (see Psalm 51:3).

Most importantly, God knew. Sin cannot be hidden from Him. He saw to it that David's cover-ups would eventually be uncovered. Moses warned the tribes that were tempted to disobey God's orders, "Behold, you have sinned against the LORD, and be sure your sin will find you out" (Numbers 32:23). We can hide sin as best we can, but it is seen by God, and He deals with it accordingly.

Therein lies the irony of it all: As human beings, we are often more concerned about what people know than with what God knows. Yet it is the divine Lawgiver who personally supervises the punishment of those who tamper with His authority. However meticulously we shield our sin from men, it is open to the eyes of God. Vividly, the author of Hebrews wrote, "And no creature is hidden from his sight, but all are naked and exposed to the eyes of him to whom we must give account" (Hebrews 4:13).

## SOME CONCLUSIONS

Even at this point in David's escapade, we can draw

some conclusions.

*Anyone can commit sexual sin*—the committed Christian as well as the casual Christian. Ministers, doctors, missionaries—all are susceptible.

A seminary professor once suggested to his students that they find a second vocation because a percentage of them would have to leave the ministry due to infidelity. Just recently, I heard of a minister who became involved with another man's wife. He was the last person I'd ever expect to be involved in such a relationship. As in so many perplexities of life, the last are often the first. Those who think they can't fall into sexual sin are often the ones who do. We must watch and pray because all of us are vulnerable.

If David, who loved God passionately, could commit adultery, we should not be surprised at our propensity to sexual sin. Though it need not happen to anyone, it *can*. Many who self-righteously said, "I never would!" must now shamefully confess, "I did."

Whenever I hear someone refer to another's failings in judgmental tones, I wince. Apart from the grace of God, we are all potential candidates for sexual misconduct.

*Passions have awesome power.* David and Bathsheba, Samson and Delilah, as well as Ahab and Jezebel are examples of the allurement of sexual desires. Our passions can exert a subtle and dictatorial power over us. We may be able to control our actions, but our minds are sometimes overtaken by sexual enticements. Unless we change our thought patterns, our firmest resolutions often collapse under the weight of sexual desire. We concur with Augustine, "There's nothing so powerful in drawing the spirit of a man downward as the caresses of a woman."[2] His own inner conflicts, which he found to be unbearable, were only resolved when he yielded himself fully to God.

Respectable husbands have abandoned their wives and children, pastors have resigned from effective ministries, and wives have left families they dearly loved all because of sexual enticement. As one said, "I hate what I'm doing, but I can't help myself. There's a part of me that wants to change, there's a part of me that doesn't. As it stands now, I think I've made the choice to go and do my own thing." In the book of Proverbs, we are warned that the one who commits sexual sin is "as an ox goes to the slaughter, or as a stag is caught fast till an arrow pierces its liver; as a bird rushes into a snare" (Proverbs 7:22–23).

I believe temptations today are greater than in previous decades. I'm told it was pornography that fueled the widespread use of the internet after it was invented. Pornography and sexually explicit movies inflame the passions and erode moral resistance. An eleven-year-old boy found a pornographic magazine in the drawer of a motel room. He became so sexually stimulated that he seduced his sister. For years he was hooked on pornography while continuing his incestuous relationship. Through God's power he has partially recovered from the experience, but his sister has not. Rebellion, bitterness, and depression have followed her into her own unsuccessful marriage.

David Morley wrote, "The sex drive is so intense that it can cut across all lines of judgment and intelligence. It can make a man cheat, steal, or kill, or make him throw away all his wealth or talent in order to pursue it."[3] Not just wealth is thrown away, but honor, influence and a Christian testimony. And it displeases the Lord. We've got latent passions that can be aroused to a fever pitch. It's like throwing a match into a can of kerosene.

*Despite the power of our passions, God holds us fully responsible for our actions.* When God sent Nathan to David, Nathan gave his message in the form of a story: There were two men in a city, one rich and the other poor. The poor man had but one little ewe lamb, yet when a traveler came to the rich man, the host stole the poor man's only lamb and prepared it for the feast (see 2 Samuel 12:1–4).

David was angry when he heard this and replied, "As the LORD lives, the man who has done this deserves to die, and he shall restore the lamb fourfold, because he did this thing, and because he had no pity" (2 Samuel 12:5–6). Nathan's response jolted David. "You are the man!" (v. 7).

David had more compassion for a lamb than he did for Uriah—another indication of how our passions distort our values. David was the man in the story who had stolen his neighbor's lamb, and God would discipline him for what he did even though it all began in a moment of unrestrained passion.

## IS GOD FAIR?

Is it right that we be judged guilty for what we really didn't intend to do? What about the responsibility of the woman, Bathsheba? Why should a man who has faithfully served the Lord for twenty years be judged harshly for one lapse in a moment of passion? And furthermore, why was Bathsheba bathing at the very moment David saw her on the rooftop? God had to know that seeing her would make David vulnerable to euphoric temptation, right?

I've heard it argued that we don't blame a dog for acting like a dog. Why should we be held accountable for doing what comes so naturally? As sexual beings, why can't we act out our sexuality?

If man were an animal, as contemporary behaviorists teach, then we must agree that humans should *not* be blamed for their actions. B.F. Skinner, who believed man *is* an animal, taught that there is no human responsibility— whatever people do, they just do. No blame should be attached to their actions.

The Bible presents a different view of humanity. Humans have a soul and mind as well as a physical body.

And because we have an eternal soul, we are not merely a cog in the machine, a victim of forces beyond our control. True, we are deeply fallen; we are born in sin and do sinful acts. In fact, we cannot change our basic corrupt nature, but we *can choose* to restrain our actions regardless of the thoughts in our mind.

David, despite the indiscretions of Bathsheba, did not *have* to commit adultery. He could have stopped staring at her as she bathed, and he could have decided against inviting her to the palace. But because he chose to sin, he was responsible.

However paralyzed we believe our wills to be in moments of temptation, we still have wills and we are accountable for our actions. The belief that we *must act on our feelings* is one of the subtle lies of passions. The bottom line: God holds us accountable to Him.

Because humanity is basically corrupt, we cannot change our inner nature. As indicated, we can refrain from certain actions, usually with great difficulty and because of overriding considerations; but God is pleased only when we do more than that. We *can choose* to cast ourselves on His mercy and ask for strength in facing moral choices. God is available to help in moments of need. Moral weaknesses should be an incentive to drive people to the cross. Christ died and rose again so that sin's grasp might be broken.

God has given us a high standard, yet with it, He has

made it possible for us to be both forgiven and morally free. Augustine, when contemplating the question of how a man can be acceptable to a holy God, said, "Give what You command, and command what You will."[4] God is not playing games with us. He expects more from us than we are capable of doing on our own, but He stands ready to help us meet His requirements.

The mercy of God is reserved for those who stop trying to give excuses for their behavior. If we take responsibility even when temptation presses us to "do it," we are in the place of humility where God can meet our deepest needs. He knows we are created from dust. He is aware of our weaknesses and our propensity to sin, yet *He cannot let us off the hook*. He is a holy God.

When we stop blaming Him and take full responsibility for what we have done, He is free to come to our aid. No excuses, no passing of the buck, no blaming God.

## WHAT ABOUT GOD?

*When we commit sexual sin, God is the loser.* When we sin, our first thought is whether we'll be punished. Will someone find out? Will God discipline us? Will we be able to cope with our guilt? Yet God is the One whom we ought to think of first. Nathan reminded David of how good God had been to him. "Thus says the LORD, the God of Israel, 'I anointed you king over Israel, and I delivered you out of the hand of Saul. And I gave you your master's house and your master's wives into your arms and gave you the house of Israel and of Judah. And if this were too little, I would add to you as much more'" (2 Samuel 12:7–8). David's sin was an act of ingratitude. His choice of Bathsheba implied that God had been negligent in meeting his needs. In effect, David was saying that the Lord's provision was not acceptable, good, and perfect. This is a reminder that every sin we commit is an indictment against God's goodness.

This attitude goes back to the Garden of Eden. Adam and Eve could freely eat of every tree except one. And what did Satan do? He blinded them to their privileges and said that if God were good and had their best interests in mind, He would let them eat of the one that was forbidden. The first sin was based on the premise that God was evil and did not, in fact, have man's best interests in mind.

Think of how good God had been to David. And God had even greater plans for him. "And if this were too little, I would add to you as much more" (2 Samuel 12:8). In one passionate act, David callously forgot God's lovingkindness. Often, sexual sin is committed against a background of multiplied privileges and blessings: good parents, an evangelical, Gospel-centered church, an understanding of the Scriptures—all these and more have been given by God, yet many have defied His Word.

Sexual immorality begins with ingratitude. The first

step to moral ruin is listed in Romans 1. "For although they knew God, they did not honor him as God or give thanks to him" (v. 21), and the rest is history. Sin and ungratefulness always go together.

Speaking of a couple who had premarital sex, Roy Hession comments, "And the greater loser in it all is God, the One whose heart was so different toward them from what they had thought, the One who was planning such good, greater than they had imagined, but whose purposes of love they have spoiled."[5]

God also loses because His reputation is tarnished. Nathan continues, "Nevertheless, because by this deed you have utterly scorned the LORD, the child who is born to you shall die" (2 Samuel 12:14). The enemies of God would be able to say, "David is like the rest of us—he talks about knowing God, but look at what he's done!" The world often makes up its mind about God based on the lives of Christians.

I'm impressed that God doesn't try to keep David's sin hidden so the enemies of the Lord might not be able to gloat over David's shame. God could have chastened David privately. News of what happened could have been confined to God's people. But God let the word spread to the pagans.

When a Christian sins, God never tries to keep it hushed up. He is willing to let His reputation be ruined in the eyes of unbelievers; God wants sin dealt with. We're the opposite. We do everything to hide our sin while God is trying to expose it.

We'll never be serious about parting with sexual sin until we know how much it grieves God. Nathan asked David, "Why have you despised the word of the LORD?" (2 Samuel 12:9). David probably didn't think of it that way, but God did.

Joseph was able to resist the daily enticements of Potiphar's wife because he was concerned with what his sin would mean to God, not to others. He could have rationalized that his family would never know if he succumbed to this beautiful woman's seduction. In the heat of the moment, he could have told himself that he deserved a bit of pleasure, considering how he was mistreated by his brothers. Couldn't he easily keep this secret from Potiphar who was gone all day? With such reasoning he might have concluded that sexual pleasure was worth the risks involved.

What kept him from sin? It was that he had a right view of sin and a right view of God; he knew the God he loved would be grieved. "How then can I do this great wickedness and sin against God?" (Genesis 39:9).

In sexual sin, both partners are hurt, but even worse, God is hurt. They are saying to Him: "You haven't been good to me. I know more than you about what is best for me. I'm not concerned about your reputation." Even when sin is skillfully hidden, God is offended; Imagine the grief of God.

## STUDY AND APPLICATION

1. Someone has said, "Idle hands are the devil's workshop." Discuss this statement in light of David's stay in Jerusalem (2 Samuel 11:1).

2. Study Psalm 32 and describe what David experienced during the time (perhaps a year) when he refused to repent of his sin.

3. In what ways are we vulnerable to sexual temptation and what can we do to minimize it?

4. Think of how our sin affects God. Can you cite instances where God expressed deep emotion because of man's sin?

5. Reread Nathan's words to David (2 Samuel 12:7–15). What thoughts did these words bring to David's mind? What is God's response to hidden sin?

CHAPTER THREE

# WHY SHOULDN'T I?

The barriers against premarital sex have all but crumbled. Adultery among consenting adults is trending. And so-called hookups among those who describe themselves as "fluid gendered" are considered normative.

Statistics tell the story: At least 33% of teenage pregnancies lead to abortions per year;[6] almost 1.5 million children are conceived out of wedlock;[7] and "of approximately 20 million new sexually transmitted infections (STIs) each year in the United States, half of cases occur among adolescents age 15–24 years."[8] And, I've already referred to all of the "consenting adults" who have extramarital affairs and who believe that sexual purity and fidelity are no longer feasible in our "advanced" society.

We've been told that the availability of contraceptives has made it possible to enjoy sex with a number of different partners without negative consequences. The progressive sexual belief of the "playboy philosophy" says you can hop from bed to bed without any ill effects. No hearts are broken, there's no rejection, no guilt, no venereal disease, or pregnancy. The more liaisons you develop, the better the chance that you will experience satisfaction and fulfillment. Millions deeply regret believing this illusion.

Young people are particularly curious: "Why is sex outside of marriage wrong? Is it really wrong, or is it wrong just because God said so?" Fair questions. Too often the impression is given that the Bible's teaching on morality has no rationale. We must follow its precepts blindly, quite apart from asking why.

I believe we ought to follow the teachings of the Bible, even if we don't understand the reason for a particular command. God knows more than we do, so we ought to submit to His authority even if it looks different from our perspective. He sees the whole picture, we don't. If time doesn't prove God correct, eternity will. Powerful reasons for chastity exist and they exist for our benefit.

## SEX IS A SPIRITUAL ACT

Paul exhorted the people of Corinth to live in sexual purity, "Or do you not know that he who is joined to a prostitute becomes one body with her? For, as it is written, 'The two will become one flesh'" (1 Corinthians 6:16). Paul is talking about the oneness that transcends the physical—the kind of spiritual unity which properly belongs to the marriage relationship.

Don't miss this: even sex with a prostitute creates a spiritual bond and they become "one flesh." This is why the first sexual act is so important—it binds you to another individual. This bond cannot be broken without guilt, mistrust, and often anger. That's why sex should be reserved for after the marriage covenant has been solemnized.

For those who believe in free love, sex is primarily a physical experience. When you're hungry you eat, when you're tired you sleep, and when you're aroused, you find a sex partner. It is this philosophy that has destroyed the character and the inner soul of those who have followed this advice.

We need some background to understand why. Thoughts are more than chemical reactions in the brain. The mind is a spiritual entity. As a pianist uses a piano to make music, so the mind uses the brain, which, in turn, affects other parts of the body through the nervous system. The brain is the key part of the body where the spiritual and physical interact. The spirit can exist independently of the brain—it is eternal.

The point? God created us so that we cannot be sexually satisfied unless we are joined to our partner spiritually as well as physically in a covenant relationship. The sex act can be pleasurable physically, but without the spiritual context, the partners, will be hurt. There must be total commitment to one person. Because of the intimacy of the sexual experience, it cannot be truly satisfying apart from being assured we belong solely to the same spouse. Hence, we have marriage of one man and one woman "till death do us part."

I've known many marriages to fall apart because the couple lived together before marriage. Later, the wife reasons, "If he talked me into going to bed with him before marriage, what would prevent him from doing the same with his secretary?" To emphasize the point: You can't have sexual satisfaction without trust, and the best way to build that trust is to postpone sex until marriage. It's commitment to the total person that makes it meaningful.

The absence or resolution of guilt is the second necessary ingredient to a complete sexual relationship. Without a clear conscience there cannot be an uninhibited *giving*, a psychological blending of the personalities. Something inside will always be unsatisfied and wrong. After Adam and Eve sinned, shame entered their relationship and the intimacy they shared was fractured. With guilt weighing on them, they turned on each other when confronted by God, and tried to pass off the blame. Adam blamed Eve, Eve blamed the serpent. And thus the history of the human race began and we have lived that out throughout the centuries: We want to hide our shame and pass blame unto others. Guilt is not a feeling that can be unlearned;

God made us in such a way that we cannot violate His laws without experiencing the uncomfortable feeling of guilt.

Of course people will tell you they don't feel guilty. Guilt often crops up disguised as depression or anger. It breeds insensitivity and frustration. As one person put it, "Even though I rationalized what I was doing, I was dying by the inch inside."

In her book, *Tough and Tender*, Joyce Landorf tells of a man who came to her husband to ask why life seemed to be so pointless. In part, he said:

> You know, Dick, I've really got it made. I'm free from the attachments of marriage. I've got this great pad at the beach and I go to bed with one sexy gal after another. I come and go as I please and I do my own thing. But something is really bothering me and I can't figure it out. Every morning as I get dressed for work I look into the mirror and think, what was last night's sexy little game all about? Sure the girl was good looking. She was good in bed and she left this morning without bugging me, but is that all there is in life? I asked myself, *"If this lifestyle is what every guy thinks he wants, why am I so depressed? Why do I feel a cold nothingness all the time?"*...I know the guys here think it would be fantastic to have this kind of liberated freedom but honestly, Dick, I hate this life.[9]

Guilt causes a psychological hesitancy in giving one's self to a partner with freedom. Mistrust and guilt smother the satisfaction of a sexual relationship.

In Genesis we read, "Adam knew Eve his wife" (Genesis 4:1). Use of the word *know* for sexual intercourse was not an attempt to camouflage the sex act in obscure language. Sexual intercourse is the highest kind of *knowing*; it's the clearest expression of psychological and emotional unity.

By contrast, animals have no spiritual dimension. Consequently, sex is purely biological for them. Animals have only physical relationships. They do what comes naturally without any questions about trust or morality. They are born and developed without the image of God; in part, that means they do not experience guilt.

## TRUST IS THE BASIS

Free love brings humans to the level of animals. Free love follows desires wherever they happen to lead without responsibility. Sex is reduced to biological pleasure. Jude refers to those who are immoral as "unreasoning animals" (v. 10). Paul wrote that God has given some over to "degrading passions" (Romans 1:26, NASB). It is the misuse of sex that dehumanizes us. It becomes purely animalistic.

That's why a married man who slept with numerous women concluded, "All that women are good for is sex. Apart from that, I wouldn't give you two bits for them."

Notice that in separating the biological from the spiritual (as one must do when living promiscuously) he saw women as existing solely to satisfy his passions. Their value as persons was irrelevant. He degraded and objectified women, but he also degraded himself.

"But," replies the anxious young man to his pastor as he sits with his arm around his girlfriend, Jan, "I am one with Jan; we have unity and trust in our relationship. Why do we have to wait until we get a marriage certificate? What good is a piece of paper anyway? The point is we plan to be married."

What good is a marriage certificate?

Throughout the years, my wife and I have lived in various places, and one move was after we purchased a house. The seller had his lawyer; we had our lawyer and Rebecca and I signed numerous papers of one kind or another. Why didn't we just shake hands and be done with it; why was "a piece of paper" (actually numerous pieces of paper!) necessary with our signatures verified?

The answer is that those pieces of paper solemnized the deal. If, the next day, we drove down another street and found a house for sale we wish we had purchased, too bad. We couldn't back out of the deal we had made; the papers we had signed committed us to the house we bought, not the one we wished we had purchased! Who pleases the Lord? One who honors the Lord and "swears to his own hurt and does not change" (Psalm 15:4).

Living together without a marriage covenant produces a conflicting message: On the one hand it says, "I like you enough to live with you;" on the other hand it says, "But I don't love you enough to be committed to you for the rest of my life." Seeds are planted that bear bitter fruit years later. Jealousy and depression are often rooted in the soil of permissiveness. Furthermore, the best rationalizations backfire.

Susan and Mike had been living together for a period of several years and now they wanted to legalize their relationship. While she was making plans for the wedding, Mike met a former girlfriend at a party. Smoldering fires were quickly ignited. He and Doris fell in love again, and within a week were in bed together. Mike called Susan on the phone to cancel the wedding or at least to postpone it until he had time to "get his head together."

Susan argued that Mike owed her marriage. After all, she had given herself to him for three years—that ought to be worth something! Mike disagreed. He admitted he had promised to marry her but didn't believe such promises were equivalent to a vow. Furthermore, the fact that they had sex together didn't obligate him to marriage. He felt he had no binding commitment to Susan, and could marry Doris.

Either way they couldn't win: To cancel the wedding

meant Susan would feel cheated; to go ahead with it meant Mike would be conned into a marriage he didn't want. Imagine the lack of excitement as such a couple approaches their wedding day. Instead of anticipating sexual intimacy and joy, they are just going through the routine of a marriage ceremony. It's like opening a present that you saw the giver buy for you.

I'm tired of hearing about sexual freedom. It's a lifestyle fraught with broken promises and empty talk about love. It's replete with feelings of guilt, selfishness, and bitter betrayal. Whatever physical pleasure is involved cannot compensate for the spiritual and emotional damage that accompanies such behavior.

As Warren Wiersbe said, "Young people are plugging their 6-volt toys into a 220-volt generator and blowing all their fuses before they have a chance to live."[10]

## TRUE LOVE SACRIFICES

In 1 Corinthians 7, Paul discusses the sexual relationship within marriage. He said, "The husband should give to his wife her conjugal rights, and likewise the wife to her husband. For the wife does not have authority over her own body, but the husband does. Likewise the husband does not have authority over his own body, but the wife does" (vv. 3–4). Note that the good of the other is to be uppermost in each partner's mind. Real love is essentially unselfish.

Casual love and real love are in sharp conflict. A natural attraction toward someone can be good in itself. We meet someone whose appearance and personality is stimulating and we enjoy their company. So far so good. But if we marry on that basis, we're apt to meet someone else who is more attractive, winsome, and sexually stimulating. Such love is subject to change because its object may lose appeal. Some marriages make it on the strength of casual love, but they are few.

## LOVE IS A COMMITMENT

The New Testament concept of love is a commitment to do what is best for the other person. Infatuation says, "I can't wait." Love says, "I will pay any price to treat you with respect. I'm willing to wait." The expression *free love* is a contradiction. If it is love, it is never free. It entails sacrifice on the part of the lover. If it's free, it's not love.

Sex, of course, is a part of married love, but it is not synonymous with love. One can exist without the other. Often couples have had sex without the slightest understanding of a loving commitment. On the other hand, it is possible to have love without sex. In the case of illness or some physical deformity, sex within the marriage may be impossible, but love can endure such strains.

Because we're born selfish, our natural tendency is to want our passions satisfied quite apart from whether it helps or hurts our partner. "I love you," a boy tells his girlfriend, but perhaps a more accurate statement would be, "I love myself, I *want* you."

What better way to prove love to someone than to forego sexual pleasure for the good of that one. After all, a man or woman's honor and good conscience are precious possessions. Why not agree to a standard and commit yourself to it at any cost?

## GUILT HAS CONSEQUENCES

The guilt associated with sexual sin can lead to anger and violence. Recently a man called me from Florida. He'd read my book, *How To Break A Stubborn Habit*. Tests, he told me, revealed he was intensely angry. On a scale of 1 to 100 he was a 96. A psychiatrist told him that he was the angriest man he had ever seen. What would cause such a man to be so frustrated and filled with rage? He had a happy home life as a child, was successful as a mechanic, and enjoyed a relatively satisfying marriage.

Soon the truth came out: He'd had some recent homosexual experiences. The guilt brought him such frustration that he wanted to lash out and commit suicide. Why? Because unresolved guilt leads to self-hatred, and self-hatred leads to hostility. This is why pornography and immorality of all kinds can lead to violence. When a criminal's apartment is searched, it almost always contains hard-core pornography and other perverse paraphernalia. I'm told that many erotic adult movies portray violence as well as explicit sex.

Police can usually tell if a murder was done by a sexual deviant because of the overkill. If the victim has numerous stab wounds instead of a half dozen, it shows that the murderer has outrageous hostility and anger. This explains why rape is not so much a crime of sex as it is a crime of violence. Anyone who is sexually unrestrained will experience such self-hatred that he will no longer care about self-respect and decency. He has acted out his sexual fantasies, so why should he not act out his desire to humiliate a woman? In a world where morality has become a matter of personal preference, what difference does it all make? To a polluted mind and conscience, anything is permissible (see Titus 1:15–16).

Abuse within our homes is reaching epidemic proportions in the United States. Many women leave home frightened because of the unpredictable rage of a hostile husband. Child abuse reports in 2021 involved over 7.2 million children.[11] Occasionally, children are even beaten to death by frustrated parents who are propelled by inflamed hostility.

Then there is sadomasochism and incest. Of sexual abuse victims that come to law enforcement's attention, more than 25% may carry the dreaded secret of sexual relationships within the family.[12] Almost always it is the result of a father who has relations with his daughter. It is impossible to calculate the inevitable fear, self-hatred, depression, and suicidal tendencies that will emerge in the life of such an abused child. No one can even estimate the number of cases that go unreported.

The connection between sexual immorality and a dead conscience capable of any act of cruelty is clearly taught in the Scriptures. Peter wrote, "And especially those who indulge in the lust of defiling passion and despise authority. Bold and willful, they do not tremble as they blaspheme the glorious ones...But these, like irrational animals, creatures of instinct, born to be caught and destroyed, blaspheming about matters of which they are ignorant, will also be destroyed in their destruction" (2 Peter 2:10, 12).

Sin is never isolated. Tolerate it in one part of our lives and it will encroach on another. If we rebel against one of God's commandments, it will be easier to violate others as well. No one has found a way to avoid sin's consequences.

## GOD'S WATCHDOG

Sexually transmitted diseases (also known as sexually transmitted infections or STIs) are God's watchdog on promiscuity. As morality spirals out of control, and promiscuity becomes the new normal, STIs are, of course, on the rise at an alarming rate, with a thirty percent increase between 2015 and 2019, and that statistic is only among those reported. In 2022, there were 2.5 million cases reported. And according to a WHO report, one million new cases are reported daily worldwide.[13] STIs have been found to be responsible for up to 40 percent of infertility issues in women.[14]

We need to understand that these diseases are associated with serious medical complications, including sterility and hazards to the health of mothers and infants. As the report on Sexually Transmitted Infections noted above states: "STIs in pregnant females will cause a higher percentage of preterm labor, premature rupture of membranes, newborns with low birth weight, chorioamnionitis, miscarriages, stillbirths, and early infant mortality....Newborns [exposed to STIs during passage through the birth canal] are at particular risk for lung and eye infections....Infants born to mothers with untreated syphilis may develop problems in many organ systems, including bones, the brain, ears, eyes, the heart, skin, and teeth."[15] Promiscuity not only affects us, but also future generations.

To further demonstrate the "normalization" of promiscuity and the transmission of STIs, there are now pharmaceuticals being touted as making one of the deadliest STIs in history, HIV/AIDS, undetectable and untransmittable in patients. But read the fine print: "Even when viral load is undetectable, HIV is still present in the body. The virus lies dormant...When therapy is halted by missing doses, taking a treatment holiday or stopping treatment, the virus emerges and begins to multiply, becoming detectable in the blood again. *This newly reproducing virus is infectious.* It is essential to take every pill every day as directed to achieve and maintain a durably undetectable status."[16]

Researchers attempt to treat these diseases as a health matter and try to normalize and destigmatize sexually transmitted infections, but it should be a matter of getting back to morality. It's one more way that society pays for its rebellion against God's established laws.

## THE LAW OF DIMINISHING RETURNS

Robert Burns wrote:

> But pleasures are like poppies spread,
> You seize the flow'r, its bloom is shed;
> Or like the snow falls in the river,
> A moment white—then melts forever.[17]

The irony of sexual misconduct, or "free love," is that there is no freedom to enjoy the satisfaction it promises. Satisfaction diminishes while desires increase. Arrive at one destination, there's always farther to go. To maintain the same erotic pleasure calls for experimenting with new thrills. That's why unbridled sex often leads to alcoholism and drugs.

The imagery of fire is used to describe unfulfilled lust. Paul spoke of those who "burned in their desire toward one another" (Romans 1:27, NASB). Quite literally, unfulfilled burning lust is a taste of hell. And just as the fires of hell are never quenched, so is the person who is consumed by lust. "Sheol and Abaddon are never satisfied, and never satisfied are the eyes of man" (Proverbs 27:20).

In his book, *Sexual Suicide*, George Gilder referred to the sexual revolution:

Erotic activity becomes a shapeless, dissolute, and destructive pursuit of ever more elusive pleasures by ever more drastic techniques. In the quest for a better orgasm or more intense titillation, a frustrated population goes on ever wilder goose chases...but always returning to the increasingly barren and shapeless lump of their own sexuality.[18]

Hell itself is compulsive desires that are unsatisfied. Fires rage within the soul but are never quenched. The rich man didn't have a single drop of water to cool his tongue (Luke 16:24). Whatever the external torments of hell, the inner fires will be worse. Those who give themselves to unbridled sensuality already know the torture of being tied to passions they both love and hate.

## WHO OWNS YOUR BODY?

Sexual temptation represents the clearest opportunity we have to declare our allegiance to Christ. Paul said, "Do you not know that your body is a temple of the Holy Spirit within you, whom you have from God? You are not your own, for you were bought with a price. So glorify God in your body" (1 Corinthians 6:19–20). He argued for sexual purity on the premise of ownership. In the Old Testament, the Shekinah glory stayed in the Holy of Holies; today, the special dwelling place of God is within Christians. To be joined to another sexually apart from marriage is unthinkable. It's like taking a pig into the Holy of Holies. Paul says it is taking the members of Christ's body and joining them to a prostitute.

There's no easy answer to sexual temptation. Our passions sometimes urge us to sacrifice the permanent on the altar of the immediate. That's why we must give up our rights to our own bodies. We have to acknowledge Christ's ownership of us—fully. Sinful pleasures are to be exchanged for other kinds of pleasures: "You make known to me the path of life; in your presence there is fullness of joy; at your right hand are pleasures forevermore." (Psalm 16:11). God has not restricted us to cheat us, but to give us a higher satisfaction.

## STUDY AND APPLICATION

1.   Carefully study 1 Corinthians 6:12–20 by answering the following questions. Using a commentary may help.

   a. Paul gives three reasons for sexual purity. Each is introduced with the question: Do you not know? State these in your own words.

   b. Why do you think immorality is different from all other sins? (v. 18)

   c. What indications are there that Paul considered sex to be a spiritual as well as a physical act?

   d. What implications do verses 19–20 have for sexual purity?

2.   Read Proverbs 7 and describe the end result of immorality.

3.   Memorize 1 John 2:15–17. List contrasts between the values of the world and the value of God's will.

4.   Study the first sin (Genesis 3). What was the nature of the deception? What are the parallels between that temptation and sexual temptation?

CHAPTER FOUR

# YES, BUT...

"I don't feel any sense of wrong when we're together...I thought I'd feel guilty, but I don't. It's a fulfilling relationship for both of us."

He looked me squarely in the eye. He had a meaningless marriage for ten years, now he's found someone who really understands him. She makes him feel like a man. As for her, she was married to an alcoholic husband, a man who had become a "great stone face," a man who simply could not communicate. There was no closeness, no warmth. Now she had found a man who was excited to share his life with her. An unhappily married man and an unhappily married woman found each other and seemed to be the fulfilment of each other's dreams. Didn't they (almost) have the right to an affair? What could be wrong with such a relationship?

Given the huge number of unhappy marriages, it's not surprising that partners meet others with whom they are better suited. The excitement of establishing a new relationship, the sense of self-worth that comes through being respected, and the exhilaration of a caring sexual relationship contribute to the feeling that it can't be all wrong.

Of course it can feel beautiful. How else can we describe a relationship between a man and a woman who understand and complement each other? Such a relationship has even been credited with preserving the sanity of a partner. A woman with an unreasonable husband told me that apart from her affair with another man, she "would have gone crazy long ago." The joy of this new relationship was like finding an oasis in a desert.

Even if the relationship is meaningful and caring, we still must ask: *At what price?*

An adulterer breaks at least five, and possibly six, of the Ten Commandments. Though the commandment, "Thou shalt not commit adultery" (Exodus 20:14, KJV) settles the issue, the question is still asked: "Is it wrong simply because God said it?" The answer is *yes*. If God is God, He has the right to determine its wrongness. In addition, adultery is intrinsically wrong because of the nature of a man and woman. God is the Creator who set up the rules by which we are to function to achieve our greatest potential. When we break the rules of our Creator, it is sin.

## GOD'S PERSPECTIVE

What other commandments does adultery break?

The commandment, "Thou shalt not bear false witness" (Exodus 20:16, KJV) reminds us of another responsibility. The marriage ceremony is an oath made in the presence of God and other witnesses. In adultery, a vow is broken; the adulterer is backing out of a solemn promise.

We hear people today say, "We're not going to have a marriage ceremony because it's so meaningless. A marriage certificate is just a piece of paper." In the previous chapter I argued that a marriage contract signified a vow and plays the same role as the contract we signed when I bought our house. No relationship exists where there is more to gain or lose than in the marriage relationship. If one walks out of the agreement, the effects are devastating.

An adulterer also bears false witness in other ways. He often lies to his wife, making up excuses for coming home late. The prophet Isaiah condemned the rebellious children who "add sin to sin" (Isaiah 30:1). When we sin and try to cover it, we multiply our offenses. God said, "Thou shalt not bear false witness" (Exodus 20:16, KJV).

A third commandment reads, "Thou shalt not steal" (Exodus 20:15, KJV). As we saw in the story of David, adultery is stealing. To take someone's wife is to steal his most precious possession.

Perhaps now we are able to understand why a sexual

relationship can be beautiful and caring, yet sinful and corrupt. The relationship may be satisfying, but the price paid when breaking God's commandments is steep. "Thou shalt not steal" is still God's standard.

## COVETING IS REBELLION

An adulterous relationship also breaks a fourth commandment, "Thou shalt not covet." Specifically, God says, "Thou shalt not covet thy neighbor's house, thou shalt not covet thy neighbor's wife, nor his manservant, nor his maidservant, nor his ox, nor his ass, nor any thing that is thy neighbor's" (Exodus 20:17, KJV). To covet means to desire something that doesn't belong to us and is basically telling God He's shortchanged us. *Coveting is rebellion against God.*

Also, God gave a commandment, "Honor thy father and thy mother" (Exodus 20:12, KJV). In almost every extramarital relationship, people dishonor their heritage and bring shame to their families.

Perhaps the most important commandment is the first, "Thou shalt have no other gods before me" (Exodus 20:3, KJV). Whenever we elevate our passions above the will of God, we have substituted our own god for the Lord God Jehovah. We are saying we have *found a pleasure more precious to us than obeying our Creator.*

That's why the Christian man who sensed no wrong in

his extramarital relationship was deceived. He thought a caring relationship could justify his actions, but he didn't realize he was shaking his fists at God in the process. Judas apparently loved silver. He betrayed Christ for thirty pieces, which he thought would satisfy his love of money. Was there anything wrong with having some extra silver? Of course not; I wish I had some myself! What made it wrong is that he denied Jesus Christ in order to get it. Adultery is evil because this sin violates Gods commandments. We can choose our lifestyle, but we cannot choose the consequences; those consequences are determined by God.

## RATIONALIZING

Consider some other rationalizations in defense of sexual misconduct.

"The way I look at it, we've all lusted in our hearts. Since lust is adultery anyway, what's the difference if I live with this divorcée?" That's the question a 35-year-old man asked after we learned he'd been having an affair with a female flight attendant. Since she was no longer married, there seemed to be less reason to become concerned about this, or so the man thought.

So, how did I reply?

It is true, of course that an adulterous heart and an adulterous act are both rebellion against God (see Matthew 5:28). But I pointed out to him that there are many differences: I shared that he has involved another person as an accomplice to his rebellion. Though all sin is basically against God (as David learned), when we invite others to join us in our sin we multiply our transgressions. The consequences of some sins are more serious than others. Lust can sometimes be forgiven without directly affecting one's relationship with others, but the sexual act cannot be easily dismissed. As we have already pointed out, because sex is a spiritual as well as a biological act, its misuse deeply tarnishes the soul. Paul wrote, "Flee from sexual immorality. Every other sin a person commits is outside the body, but the sexually immoral person sins against his own body" (1 Corinthians 6:18). Think about the consequences: broken vows, broken marriages, and broken lives.

Those who engage in a sex act must bear greater consequences than those who sin only in the mind. It's simply not true to say that if we've done one (sinned in the mind), we might as well do the other (sinned in the flesh).

*Don't I deserve happiness?* "I have a right to happiness... this is probably my only chance. Furthermore, I should never have married this person in the first place. So, why can't I have this relationship? I deserve it."

The Declaration of Independence states that we have a right to "Life, Liberty and the pursuit of Happiness," but this doesn't mean we are entitled to pursue happiness by any means possible. We have a right to pursue happiness only by lawful means. Apparently, the partner being sinned against has no right to happiness, nor do the children. I cannot pursue happiness unlawfully unless someone else relinquishes their right to happiness. Roy Hession wrote about adultery:

> Someone else paid the price of losing his life-companion; somebody else has shed tears far into the night; somebody else has been robbed of his happiness; somebody else has had his home broken up; somebody else has been left lonely, struggling along on his own; children have been left without a father or a mother. It is easy to forget the terrible wrongs another has suffered as we enjoy our new love.[19]

C.S. Lewis observed that the principle of pursuing happiness by immoral means "once allowed in that department, must sooner or later seep through our whole lives. We thus advance toward a state of society in which not only each man but every impulse in each man claims carte blanche."[20]

Can someone be happy while grieving the Spirit of God? What if Christ had bypassed the torture of the cross in the pursuit of His own happiness? Pascal commented wisely, "Happiness is neither out of us nor in us. It is in God." We have an obligation to obey God and worship

Him, but we are not obligated to be happy. "A right to happiness doesn't, for me, make much more sense than a right to be six feet tall, or to have a millionaire for your father, or to get good weather whenever you want to have a picnic."[21] No one has a right to pursue happiness at the expense of moral character. We have even less right to do it in defiance of God.

What about the argument, "I should never have married this person in the first place"?

Have we forgotten that God specializes at working in, through, and in spite of our mistakes and failures? No one blew it as badly as Adam and Eve. They had a perfect opportunity to obey, but their unbelief brought devastation to the whole human race. God did not let them evade responsibility. After they sinned so directly and intentionally, He promised to meet their need right where they were. The past cannot be redone, but the future is not the end of the story.

God's solution to one sin (a foolish marriage) is never for us to commit a second sin (to find some reason to break our marriage vow). He's more concerned about changing us than our circumstances. Patience within marriage is more honorable than seeking an exit from it. When we repent of sin, God uses those experiences to build maturity in us. Of course where there is abuse or an adulterous partner, the marriage vow may be formally broken. The issue of divorce is controversial and must be pursued by council of one's church leadership.

Some rationalize that *it's possible to sin moderately and be satisfied.* "I'd never go to bed with a woman, but I do look at porn." A person thinks they're able to draw a line beyond which they won't go—believing they're quite safe in their own private world. I'm also thinking of the person who watches sexually explicit movies or reads erotic novels. They're the kinds of people who sin vicariously. They wouldn't commit adultery, but they watch illicit shows and identify with people who commit adultery or are sexually promiscuous. They may envy the path of the wicked, but so far they've stayed within the folds of the church—except of course in their private minds.

Let's remind ourselves that the more we feed our sinful nature, the stronger it becomes. Consider an alcoholic who believes they can stop drinking at any time—and often can, but their appetite for alcohol grows steadily until they're not be able to say *no* regardless of how badly they wish to.

So it is with sensuality: It may begin with pornography or a sexually explicit scene, but soon it will lead to sexual acts. It's like feeding a hungry baby tiger. He's manageable now, but he will grow to become a ferocious beast. One young person said, "I thought if I went to see one X-rated movie I'd get all of the curiosity out of my system, but now I'm hooked."

Christ flatly denied that it's possible to sin and yet be in control of the situation. To commit sin is to be the slave of it (see John 8:34). I've heard of people drifting in a boat on the salty ocean who became so thirsty that they insisted on drinking ocean water even though they'd been warned not to do so. The water looked great and they were convinced it would slake their thirst. What they didn't realize was that a half cup of salt water would increase their thirst several times over. They would die of thirst sooner than those who restrained themselves and waited to be rescued. There is no such thing as taking a little bit of salt water and being satisfied.

Many years ago, when he was Prime Minister of England, Oliver Cromwell attended a circus. An animal trainer came onto the imitation grass, cracked his whip, and a huge snake wrapped itself around his body. When the crowd hushed at the spectacle, they suddenly heard bones cracking. The animal trainer soon was dead. He had trained the snake for fourteen years—from the time he got it when it was only seven inches long. Back then, the trainer could have crushed it between his forefinger and thumb. Because he thought he had it under his control, he believed he was safe with the grown snake. He was quite wrong.

God's Word assures us that we can never keep sin contained. If we willfully yield to it, it will inevitably demand more until, at last, we are consumed by it.

Whatever we rationalize, we must ask God to show us why it's a lie. For the flesh and the devil, deception is the name of the game. We should actually fear sin, knowing we can become ensnared when we play with it.

You've heard it said that "the fear of the Lord" refers to reverencing God, and so we don't have to be afraid of Him. I was surprised to find that can't be proved biblically! Read passages such as Deuteronomy 6:13–15, where the fear of the Lord is directly linked to His anger and punishment. Even believers, who are secure in the eternal love of God, must have a proper fear of God. In other words, the word fear means *fear!*

How does God discipline us? By letting sin have more control over us. He gives us what we crave and more besides. The greater the rebellion to God, the greater the slavery to sin.

We may say that nobody understands our situations. Maybe they don't, but God does. Though He loves us deeply, He never changes His mind about sin just because we're in a tough spot. He wants us to give up our rationalizations, regardless of the cost.

## STUDY AND APPLICATION

1. Proverbs 6:26–35 describes the sin of adultery. What other sins accompany adultery? What are the consequences listed?

2. Read Deuteronomy 6:4–9. Why do you think Satan would be so concerned about destroying homes? Why is adultery such an attractive means to this end?

3. Study Hebrews 13:4. What does the verse teach about marriage?

4. Read Revelation 18:2–8. By what standard does God judge the harlot Babylon? Does this teach us anything about the sufferings of eternal hell?

CHAPTER FIVE

# I'LL TAKE MY CHANCES

"I know chastity is right, but is it smart?" the young man wanted to know. "God may say immorality is wrong, but even so, maybe a man is cheating himself out of euphoric pleasure for no really important reason," he continued. "Tell me the worst that could happen if I go ahead with it." He was weighing the pros and cons. His reasoning was straight forward: As long as the price wasn't too high, he would disregard God's opinion. Sure, he might have to pay for his sin, but if he could control the consequences, he might get by rather cheaply. There are bargains everywhere—maybe he could find one for his sexual relationship. The forbidden pleasure may well be worth the price. He thought he'd take his chances.

Is disobedience ever worth the price? Must we always pay for sin or can we simply ignore the consequences and do our own thing? But think about it: If the pleasure of sin would, even in one instance, compensate for the consequences, God would be rewarding sin, and that's something He never does.

We've all become accustomed to credit cards and apps, which make it possible to enjoy almost anything now and pay later. The problem is that we *do* have to pay, and sometimes at exorbitant interest rates. We can't have the enjoyment without the slavery.

Sin is deceptive for three reasons. *First, it pays some immediate dividends.* Let's be honest and admit there is pleasure in sin. If sin wasn't enjoyable, the road of sensuality wouldn't be so well-traveled. This means a lot to the *now* generation where immediacy is all that counts. "I'll sin today and deal with the devil tomorrow" has led many a person permanently down a destructive path.

*Sin also deceives us because most of its consequences are hidden.* James wrote, "But every man is tempted, when he is drawn away of his own lust, and enticed" (James 1:14, KJV). The expression "drawn away" has the idea of baiting a trap. A hunter leaves a chunk of fresh meat on the trap which is concealed in the snow. There are some immediate rewards for the bear who comes strolling by because the meat tastes good. But all the ugly consequences are hidden from view.

The word *enticed* is used of baiting a hook. Again, there is both immediate gratification and concealment of the consequences. The fish is promised something appealing without understanding what it's going to cost him. Since animals and fish are ignorant of how traps and hooks work, they are caught. They have no idea that suffering and death await them.

Similarly, it's easy to fantasize about the most exotic sexual experience and even be able to enjoy it temporarily as long as we are blind to what's happening to ourselves and to others; but God is grieved because of our disobedience.

*Sin is deceptive because it appears controllable.* Whenever we get by with our sin, we develop confidence in our own ability to control our passions. An unmarried couple may think they are able to stop before sexual intercourse, and maybe they can. But every time they overstep God's boundaries, their consciences are deadened and their defenses weakened. Even if they pride themselves in their technical chastity, they're bound to find other sins in their lives that are out of control. A double-minded man is unstable in all his ways (James 1:8).

One man, determined to brave heaven and hell to get what he wanted, said, "But you've got to admit that David did get his Bathsheba despite his sin!" True. And Samson get his Delilah, and Judas his silver. But think of how much they paid!

In Galatians 6:7 we read, "Do not be deceived: God is not mocked, for whatever one sows, that will he also reap." Paul warns us against deception or thinking we can find some loophole in God's way of dealing with the world. It's foolish to think we can actually bypass the knowledge and opinion of God!

## WE REAP WHAT WE SOW

Let's consider three laws of sowing and reaping. Sow wheat and you get wheat; sow corn and you get corn. Sin always reproduces more sin. Sometimes it is more of the same sin; sometimes it is different sins. The works of the flesh come in clusters; they tend to spawn other forms of disobedience. David began with adultery and ended with murder. The principle applies to other sins as well. Dishonesty begets more dishonesty. Greed leads to stealing once, and not getting caught, which leads one to try it again. Each time the grip becomes stronger. And stealing leads to lying, lying to cheating, and the list continues.

How does God discipline His children when they sin? We usually expect Him to send a bolt of lightning. Or perhaps we think He permits accidents or terminal illness. I think God often *gives us more of what we want.* One immoral act leads to another, which in turn leads to another, but along with the enjoyment comes greater slavery.

Remember when the children of Israel cried to God for meat? They hated the menu in the desert. Like gluttons today, they were insisting they should have more tasty foods, more selection, and a cafeteria of options. God became upset with their luxurious desires and said, "You shall not eat just one day, or two days, or five days, or ten days, or twenty days, but a whole month, until it comes out at your nostrils and becomes loathsome to you, because you have rejected the LORD who is among you and have wept before him, saying, 'Why did we come out of Egypt?'" (Numbers 11:19–20).

God's discipline for His people wanting meat was to give them an overabundance of it! No doubt they enjoyed the meat for a while, but soon it became disgusting. Those enticed by the thrills of sensuality later discover they're bound by what they have now come to hate.

One sure sign of complete repentance is when we are afraid to fall back into our old sins, lest God judge us with even greater slavery. A person who had gained victory over his alcoholism told me that he would never take so much as one drink again. He's afraid the cycle of bondage will start all over again. He has finally understood a basic principle: Whatever we sow, we reap.

## WE REAP IN A DIFFERENT SEASON

Have you ever noticed how casual people are about sin? One of the reasons we have so many divorces among Christians is because we see those who left their spouses for other partners and now appear to be well-adjusted and happy. It seems as if God isn't as strict as He used to be. Maybe some of the consequences aren't happening anymore.

"Because God does not punish sinners instantly, people feel it is safe to do wrong" (Ecclesiastes 8:11, TLB). I don't know why God is so patient with disobedience. He doesn't settle His accounts at the end of the month. He's willing to wait for the wild oats to ripen. If we entertain any doubts about God, we should remember that He never changes. He hates sin as much as ever.

We can liken a sinful lifestyle to a smorgasbord—progressively taking whatever we want and paying for it in the end. Of course the bills come due, then our character is eroded. The heart condemns (1 John 3:21), joy and assurance of God's guidance evaporate, relationships rupture. All this for the pleasure of sin. And that's not the end. The remote consequences are a wasted life with no works able to survive the fire of God's judgment. Even for believers, the results of disobedience are priced right out of sight.

Think of all the children who are confused, hurt, and rejected because of an unfaithful mother or an alcoholic father. Consider the wasted life, the misguided values, the suspicion and hatred that sin brings in its wake. We have only a sliver of time on Earth in comparison to endless eternity, yet God will judge us for how we spend these brief years, and what we've done, for good or for ill, will go on for eternity.

I'm convinced many people will have to wait until they're in eternity before they believe that God was right, that sin is as bad as God says it is. The consequences are built right into the nature of sin and cannot be bypassed. God has promised, "Whoever conceals his transgressions will not prosper, but he who confesses and forsakes them will obtain mercy" (Proverbs 28:13).

God's patience is not an indication that the sinner is getting by with the wrong they're committing.

## WE REAP MORE THAN WE SOW

As a boy out on our farm, I learned that one kernel of wheat could produce as many as thirty kernels during a time of harvest. David learned that consequences of sin sometimes boomerang. He thought he could keep his sin a secret, but God had other thoughts about David's immoral ways. God told David, "For you did it secretly, but I will do this thing before all Israel and before the sun" (2 Samuel 12:12). Later David's son Absalom committed immorality in view of everyone. David thought he could keep it secret, but God said He would personally see to it that all would become public.

David had said that the man who stole the sheep should pay fourfold. He didn't know he was speaking about himself. Four of his sons died prematurely. First, Bathsheba's son died. Second, Amnon raped his sister Tamar. Then Amnon was killed by Absalom because of this crime. Absalom was later killed because he wanted to take the throne from David. And finally, Adonijah was executed because he wanted to become king. In the end, David came back into fellowship with God, but his children didn't.

Sin is like yeast—a little bit leavens the whole lump. Its influence is much greater than its size or shape, and its consequences are unpredictable. No wonder we need a Redeemer to get us out of the mess! Trying to do it ourselves is like attempting to mop the floor while the sink is overflowing and the faucet is still running. God wants us to understand that sin is a high-priced item. Charles G. Finney wrote, "Sin is the most expensive thing in the universe. Nothing else can cost so much. Pardoned or unpardoned, its cost is infinitely great. Pardoned, the cost falls chiefly on the great atoning substitute; unpardoned, it must fall on the head of the guilty sinner."[22]

Again, Finney has written, "How many tears, poured out like water, it has cost; how much pain in many forms this enterprise has caused and cost; yea, that very sin which you roll as a sweet morsel under your tongue! God may well hate it when He sees how much it costs and say 'Oh do not do that abominable thing that I hate!'"[23]

The idea that we can sin and take our chances began

in the Garden of Eden. Eve thought she could satisfy her sensual appetite and actually enhance her own status (see Genesis 3:6). Was it really a reasonable gamble? If it didn't work out, she might have thought she could return to her original state, but the devastation that sin brought could never have been predicted. Throughout all eternity, multitudes will be in torment because Adam and Eve disobeyed God.

Let's review what I call the cycle of disobedience.

*First,* we are in control. We set the limits of disobedience.

*Second,* we win some battles, are able to restrain ourselves, and have the feeling of being in complete command of the situation. Because we successfully restrained ourselves, we may believe we can stop the cycle of disobedience whenever we want. However, if we should miss some forbidden pleasures, we stay in the vicinity of the temptation.

*Third,* we weigh the pros and cons and conclude that the fulfillment of our selfish desires outweighs any consequences we can foresee, and thus, we tell ourselves we have made a wise choice.

*Fourth,* we sign the contract. We commit ourselves to certain lifestyles, believing there are exceptions—but only just for us.

*Fifth,* the terms of the agreement are suddenly changed. Just like Gehazi who thought he was getting gold, but ended up with leprosy (2 Kings 5:22–27); we realize that we didn't read the fine print. Suddenly we're not in control and when we try to get out of our dilemma, we find our agreement is binding.

*Sixth*, Satan comes to collect. We can't believe what's happening. It's out of our hands.

*Seventh*, we are absolutely desperate and we ask God for a quick deliverance.

But God won't bail us out until we've learned our lesson. Those who work with alcoholics say there's no use trying to help them until they "bottom out." They've got to come to the end of themselves *totally*. By experience, they must be convinced of the high cost of drink.

Have you ever heard one caught in sin's grip say, "If I had only known"? What they're actually saying is, "If I had only believed God." Every deliberate sin is a choice against the guidance and goodness of God.

If we say, "I've learned to live with my guilt," we're actually saying, "I have learned to live in defiance of God."

## STUDY AND APPLICATION

1. What is the thrust of 1 Timothy 5:6?

2. Read Titus 1:15. What are the effects of a polluted mind and conscience?

3. In light of John 8:34, discuss the idea that we can sin deliberately and still be in control.

4. Contrast the way the world looks at the pleasures of sin with Paul's evaluation (Titus 3:3).

5. Apply to the United States (or any country) the three laws of sowing and reaping in this chapter.

ERWIN W. LUTZER

## CHAPTER SIX

# BUT, I CAN'T LET HER GO

"Sure it's sin. I've tried—God knows I have—but, I can't let her go."

His final words caught my attention. They came at the end of a long discussion with a man about his wife's failures and a concealed affair with a woman he truly loved. He said the words slowly and deliberately. "But, I can't let her go."

Being unable to let go also applies to other sins such as drug and alcohol addiction, pornography, gluttony, and so on, but breaking a relationship with another human being is even more difficult. There has been a sharing of intimacies; promises made, emotions enflamed. For those in meaningless marriages, the letting go of an affair is unthinkable. Widows and widowers find intimate companionship so enticing and that it can be so fulfilling, it leads to sexual liaisons. The death of a partner or a divorce creates a vacuum for a partner that can be fulfilled only through sexual closeness (or so it is claimed). To suggest otherwise brings the objection, "You don't understand!"

Yet God asks that the cherished desires of the heart be laid to rest. He knows that we are not at the mercy of our feelings, regardless of how loudly our passions protest. In the Scriptures we read, "No temptation has overtaken you that is not common to man. God is faithful, and he will not let you be tempted beyond your ability, but with the temptation he will also provide the way of escape, that you may be able to endure it" (1 Corinthians 10:13).

Consider Christ's startling statement: "But I say to you that everyone who looks at a woman with lustful intent has already committed adultery with her in his heart" (Matthew 5:28). With such a high standard, all men are indicted! Lust is lodged in every human heart. How can such desires be brought under control? Christ anticipated our response. He knows that parting with lust is like getting rid of a part of our bodies.

So Jesus continued: "If your right eye causes you to stumble, gouge it out and throw it away. It is better for you to lose one part of your body than for your whole body to be thrown into hell. And if your right hand causes you to stumble, cut it off and throw it away. It is better for you to lose one part of your body than for your whole body to go into hell." (Matthew 5:29–30, NIV). The term *stumbling block* according to William Barclay, means "bait-stick in a trap." The picture is that of a pit dug in the ground and

LIVING WITH YOUR PASSIONS

deceptively covered with a thin layer of branches carefully arranged so the unwary traveler would step on it and fall into the pit. Jesus is saying that if your eye or hand causes you to be tripped up—if you find yourself tempted sexually—take drastic action.

It is often through the eye—a look—that lust begins. Then, perhaps, tender words intensify the desire, and gentle caresses open up the floodgates of passion. According to Jesus, if it is necessary to cut off a hand or to pluck out an eye to keep sexually pure—do it! Unfortunately, many might try to dismiss His words, arguing that He was speaking figuratively or that getting rid of one eye or hand is no safeguard; we have two eyes and two hands.

Though Jesus was not telling us to amputate parts of our bodies, He expects us to take action—to cut off the source of our lust or remove ourselves from the temptation. He recognized striking parallels between parting with members of our bodies and saying *no* to our passions. He understood that both require extraordinary measures. Notice these parallels.

## AMPUTATION IS PAINFUL

Sitting here in my study, I'm trying to visualize my right arm amputated; even worse, having my right eye removed. The thought is abhorrent. In ancient times, there was no anesthetic, no way to alleviate the throbbing torment that accompanied surgery. No needles, helpful drugs, or delicate surgical instruments—just crude cutting tools. Grotesque scars remained as reminders of the ordeal. In our day, anesthetics deaden the pain. It may be excruciating once the anesthetic wears off, but there is hope for recovery. Wounds heal and strength returns.

Jesus knew we highly prize our hands and eyes; we'd do anything to spare them. We wouldn't part with them unless our life was at stake. Lust is as difficult to part with as a hand or an eye. Anyone who has experienced the exhilaration of sexual attraction knows that. Consider the man who is dreaming about his wrongful lover. Happiness (it appears) is within his grasp, yet he must say *no* when the prize is within his reach.

I once spoke to a man who was in love with another woman, but they decided to break off their relationship so he could go back to his wife and family and rebuild a deteriorating marriage. He still had deep affection for the woman and wondered why his emotions didn't change toward his wife. A healing process must take place, just as when a marriage partner dies. There will be grief, tears, and loneliness. Who can understand such emotional pain, yet Christ says, "Do it."

How?

First by getting away from the temptation. Paul's advice is, "Flee from sexual immorality" (1 Corinthians

6:18). And again, "So flee youthful passions" (2 Timothy 2:22). Run from temptation without leaving a forwarding address.

What if temptation is close—next door or at the job? The seed of sensuality must be crushed before it gets an opportunity to become firmly rooted in mind and body. Whatever it takes, stop it—it is sin sweetly poisoned.

Theaters, bars, and similar places appeal to fleshly desires. Break off any relationships that have become doorways to allurement. It may be necessary to change jobs. Eliminate access to websites that host pornography and provocative movies, and part company with friends who influence you to do evil (see Proverbs 1:10–19).

"There's no way I can escape temptation," you say. "It's where I work, and even changing jobs wouldn't guarantee immunity from further enticement."

True, but that doesn't negate Christ's words. We often know precisely what we could do to counteract the inroads into our private world of passion.

We must ask God to "lead us not into temptation." We are confronted daily with sin in a hundred different disguises. God can direct us to avoid the pitfalls; He can keep us from stumbling. If we ask Him, He will shield us from circumstances in which we are particularly vulnerable. "The Lord knows how to rescue the godly from trials, and to keep the unrighteous under punishment until the day of judgment" (2 Peter 2:9).

When we flee, we have God on our side.

We must fling the stumbling block aside, treat it as a woman would a mugger. It is not the time for sweet negotiations and a drawn-out farewell. We should never treat sin with compassion or compromise. Saying no to our passions is painful but possible. Many have had an eye removed or an arm amputated when gangrene has set in. They endured the suffering to contain the poison. Jesus knew it wouldn't be easy, yet He asked us to do it for our own good and for His name's sake.

## AMPUTATION IS THOROUGH

Suppose you go to a doctor with a cancerous growth on your arm and he says, "I plan to do this in stages. I'll cut out most of it this time and take more later. We won't decide now whether we will eventually take it all."

Absurd? Of course. You want him to cut a trifle beyond the growth to make sure he's got it all. You want the surgery to be final. Once the decision has been made, you can't rethink it. This should also be true of sexual sin. Benjamin Needler, a Puritan writer, put it this way: "We must not part with sin, as with a friend, with a purpose to see it again and to have the same familiarity with it as before, or possibly greater....We must shake our hands of it as Paul did shake the viper off his hand into the fire."[24]

How can this be applied? We are to burn every bridge behind us—no turning back (remember Lot's wife). Just as the ancient Jews searched their houses with a candle to be sure there was no leaven left among them, we must, with the same diligence, search our lives lest there be a bit of poison that deadens our whole body. Pull it out, even if it resists like a tooth in the jaw.

What opens the door to sexual vulnerability? Television? Movies? Websites? Fantasizing about another's wife or husband? In Romans we read, "But put on the Lord Jesus Christ, and make no provision for the flesh, to gratify its desires" (Romans 13:14).

When I speak of making a complete break with sin, I don't mean just sexual sin. *Any sin* we tolerate can be the cause of failure in sexual temptations. Paul taught that immorality, impurity, sensuality, idolatry, sorcery, and other sensual sins have a common root: the flesh (see Galatians 5:19–21). Compromise in one matter leads to problems in another. Unresolved anger can lead to drunkenness; dishonesty to immorality.

Any counselor knows cause-effect relationships in behavior are skillfully hidden. Why are we overcome by the same sin again and again? Often, it's because we haven't probed deeply enough; we may be denying God access to all areas of life. This is illustrated by a remarkable story in Joshua 7. Israel was routed when fighting the men of

Ai. Joshua and his army lost 36 men in the skirmish. If a military expert were to analyze the cause of the debacle, what would he say? He'd evaluate the army, study its tactics, and recommend sophisticated equipment along with a better strategy. He'd give a timetable for beefing up the Israelite war machine so that the enemy would be subdued quickly and with a minimum of casualties.

Actually, the strength of Israel's army had little to do with its defeat or victory. The real cause was that Achan had stolen a garment which was to have been destroyed along with the city of Jericho. No secular man could make such an analysis. On the surface, there was no connection between a stolen garment and a defeated army, but God established such connections.

Because of the common root of sin (rebellion), one sin, however distantly related, can be the cause of another. The forces that open the heart's door to lust may be fed from a different source.

A man who could not overcome the habit of watching pornography found that sin's power was broken when he thoroughly repented of other sins which he had conveniently overlooked. These included returning stolen items, asking his parents to forgive his rebellion, and confessing his anger at God for his predicament in life. Also—and this is important—overcoming any addiction is best done by bonding with other believers to pray, support one another, and hold each other accountable.

You might not think cheating on your income tax can lead to failing in sexual temptation, but it can. If covetousness caused a military defeat, it can cause a moral defeat as well. That's why some types of sensual, degrading music can lead to immorality, violence, guilt, and anger. Ultimately, all sin is related and has consequences that to us might seem random. A.W. Tozer wrote, "That part of ourselves that we rescue from the Cross may be a very little part of us, but it is likely to be the seat of our spiritual troubles and our defeats."[25]

Take an unhurried half hour and pray with the psalmist, "Search me, O God, and know my heart! Try me and know my thoughts! And see if there be any grievous way in me, and lead me in the way everlasting!" (Psalm 139:23–24).

## AMPUTATION IS WORTHWHILE

Is the pain worth it? Ask the cancer patient who has been told by his doctor, "We got it all!" The exhilaration of a physical cure fades in comparison with the advantages of moral freedom. Jesus said that if in a choice between losing an eye or losing the soul, it would be foolish to choose to keep the eye and forfeit one's soul (Matthew 5:30). The soul is worth infinitely more. To ruin the soul through guilt and shame (even if the person is eventually saved) is a high price to pay for forbidden pleasure. Christian Bovee said,

"The body of a sensualist is the coffin of a dead soul."[26]

The handicapped man with only one hand and one eye is unable to fulfill his cherished dreams. The hopes of a lifetime are shattered. He really has no option except to adjust to a host of unfulfilled wishes and desires. He'll have to bury his plans and redirect his life toward simpler goals. He'll either readjust or self-destruct.

Christ knows our disappointments. Yet, He says, "It is *better* to live without companionship than to have it in defiance of God. It's preferable to go through life with a tumultuous marriage and be able to claim God's friendship than to be fulfilled and incur God's disfavor. God is a friend of the lonely, frustrated, and tempted; but He will judge those who commit immorality." As Hebrews 13:4 clearly says, "For God will judge the sexually immoral and adulterous."

Walter Trobisch spoke with insight, "The task we have to face is the same, whether we are married or single: to live a fulfilled life in spite of many unfulfilled desires."[27]

Sexual sin, however appealing, is never worth more than an arm or an eye. Someone has said, "How prompt we are to satisfy the hunger and thirst of our bodies; how slow to satisfy the hunger and thirst of our souls." And somewhere I read this bit of advice: When we have to jump over a chasm, it's better to do it in one long jump rather than in two short ones! We need to obey instantly—whatever the cost.

## BREAKING THE RELATIONSHIP

Let's return to the man who said, "But, I can't let her go." He and the woman he met appear to be perfectly suited, but God has said *no*. A feeling of indebtedness has developed. They've voluntarily given themselves to the most intimate of all relationships, and the woman may say to him, "If you leave me, I'll commit suicide—you're the only person in the world who understands me." Or she may say, "If you leave me, I'll spread it all over town. I'll slander you—you've got more to lose than I do."

What can the man do?

He can approach her in a spirit of humility and confess his part of the sin. It's useless to argue who is responsible; to a lesser or greater degree, assuming it was consensual, both are accountable. He should help her see that he is genuinely sorry that he robbed her of intimacy—he stole what he did not own and took a path that leads to destruction. He can tell her that this is the end. It's final.

He should be willing to submit to any discipline the Lord might allow. Fear of exposure must not prevent confessing and forsaking sin. Any adulterous relationship is a defiling bond that has the power to paralyze you, make you slave to that person, and start a spiral into deeper sin. The detour is always rougher than the main road. Whatever happens, it will likely be less serious than losing an eye or a hand. No one has succeeded in making the way of the transgressor easy.

Yes, you can let her go.

## STUDY AND APPLICATION

1. In light of 2 John 6, what does a person's willingness to put away sin say about his love for God?

2. Does God ever ask believers to do the impossible? If not, how do we receive the enablement to do what we should?

3. Since the eyes are usually involved in sexual temptation (Matthew 5:28), what practical steps are necessary to keep ourselves pure? How can Christians help one another in this?

4. If a someone falls in love with someone else's spouse, what steps can be taken to *rebuild* the existing marriages?

5. In Genesis 22, we have an example of a man who was willing to set aside all human affection to do the will of God. What blessings did he receive as a result of obedience?

CHAPTER SEVEN

# IS IT OKAY IF
# I DO IT BY MYSELF?

Possibly one of the most widespread sexual practices especially among young people is sexual self-gratification. As has been said, "No other form of sexual activity has been so frequently discussed, so roundly condemned and more universally practiced, than masturbation."[28] The guilt associated with this practice is often excessive. I once received a letter that read, "Please help me...I masturbate. Is there any hope? I've even thought of suicide."

Christian teachers that I respect have landed on different sides of this issue. A few generations ago, masturbation was almost unanimously condemned by Christian counselors and pastors. But times have changed. Today, some Christian youth leaders tell young people that it isn't a sin unless done too frequently. James Dobson says that unless it is done excessively or as a substitute for intimacy in marriage, it should be accepted as a normal part of growing up.[29]

Several arguments favor this approach. Almost every

young man, and a good percentage of young women have, at some time, practiced masturbation. Whatever struggles a person may have with it, they can at least be assured that it's often a normal part of adolescent development.

Also, most expressions of this behavior have no harmful physical effects. Contrary to the dire warnings of past generations, it does not produce insanity or make one more susceptible to disease. Such fears, which were intended to discourage the practice, were ill founded.

However, perhaps the most oft repeated argument in favor of a more relaxed attitude is that masturbation is usually accompanied by excessive and destructive guilt. The logic is obvious: some would say, "If it is accepted as an expected sexual outlet, the guilt will vanish." Or so it is thought.

Although the Bible condemns all kinds of sexual sin, it makes no explicit reference to masturbation. The Bible does refer implicitly to nocturnal emissions as unclean. However, the physiological response had a cleansing process similar to the cleaning of a woman's period (see Leviticus 15:16–19). The purpose of cleansing was most probably for public sanitation and to set apart the marriage bed as holy. Also the expression, "abusers of themselves with mankind" (1 Corinthians 6:9, KJV), is a reference to homosexuality. Since there are references to masturbation in Egyptian literature (1500–1000 BC), its omission could not be because it was unknown. Considering all of the detailed laws in the book of Leviticus, it's remarkable that it's not mentioned anywhere. Possibly, God did not want to lay a burden on us that was too heavy to bear.

Before masturbation is dismissed as a harmless release of sexual energy, we dare not ignore the warnings of Scripture, such as, "Beloved, I urge you as sojourners and exiles to abstain from the passions of the flesh, which wage war against your soul" (1 Peter 2:11). Paul taught that we should keep our minds from thinking evil. "Finally, brothers, whatever is true, whatever is honorable, whatever is just, whatever is pure, whatever is lovely, whatever is commendable, if there is any excellence, if there is anything worthy of praise, think about these things" (Philippians 4:8).

Even when practiced infrequently, masturbation is most often accompanied by sexual fantasies, which fall under the general category of lust or covetous desire. Those who are told it isn't sinful may experience less guilt, but many still admit that they have a sense of shame or at least defeat. Interestingly, though other kinds of sexual behaviors are talked about freely in our society, and some people may claim without shame that they live immorally, masturbation still causes many a sense of embarrassment. Walter and Ingrid Trobisch published their correspondence with a girl named Ilona who was struggling with the practice. She wrote, "On the surface masturbation is something beautiful for me which I want to experience.

But deep down it is a burden. Every time that I give in I feel guilty even though no one ever forbade me to do it."[30] Masturbation involves taking a gift designed by God to establish an intimate relationship with one's spouse and using it selfishly. It's aborting the development of a caring and communicating relationship.

For some, the habit leads to enslavement. Though it may be a temporary release of sexual tension, it can eventually inflame the passions. Sometimes it's like using oil to put out a fire. Some practice it several times a day unable to free themselves from the addiction.

Excessive masturbation is often a symptom of a deeper problem which may not be sexual. Sensuality grows best in the soil of a self-indulgent life: overeating, oversleeping, avoiding difficult challenges, etc. It may also be symptomatic of deeper unresolved spiritual problems.

For example, a person who is angry because they believe they have been shortchanged in life may masturbate thinking, "Considering what I've got to put up with, I deserve this little bit of pleasure." It then becomes a compensation for the discouragements of life, and one's dependency on it grows. As Ilona wrote, "Usually deep down, there is a feeling of dissatisfaction with one's self and with one's life, which one tries to overcome in a short moment of pleasure. But one does not succeed. The desired satisfaction is not reached."[31]

If an individual is angry with God, their spouse, or their job, these issues must be faced before masturbation can be overcome. If not, they will not only lack the desire to change, but they'll take the path of least resistance and fall back into the habit. It's the "What's-the-use-anyway?" feeling that tends to dampen any motivation for change.

When the Bible says the power of sin is in the Law, it implies we are under sin's dominion because of its condemnation (1 Corinthians 15:56). As long as there is a sense of defeat or self-hatred, it's hard to keep up the fight.

Because our sexuality is so intimately connected with the very core of our being, masturbation generates shame as well as guilt. That's why it can become such a major stumbling block in our spiritual growth. And the more it becomes the focus of the mind's attention, the more powerful it seems to become.

Although, in one sense, all sin is sin, there's no doubt that some sins are greater than others. Jesus condemned the Pharisees because they tithed but neglected the weightier matters of the Law (Matthew 23:23). Self-righteousness is more heinous to God, but because it isn't linked to sexual immorality, it may generate little guilt. Yet such sins of the spirit are also just as abhorrent to God as the sins of the flesh. Not for a moment should we excuse sensual sins, but sometimes we lose our perspective when we're in the midst of the struggle.

The answer then is not to condone masturbation. It seems unlikely that it can be done without the accompanying sin of lust, nor in faith—and Paul taught that whatever was not of faith was sin (Romans 14:23). Rather, it must be considered as a fleshly habit God wants the person to overcome, even as the struggle continues.

As for the guilt, there is an excellent cure. Our conscience can be cleansed and we can be at peace with God even while we struggle to overcome various sins and failures. When the Scriptures promise, "If we confess our sins, he is faithful and just to forgive us our sins and to cleanse us from all unrighteousness" (1 John 1:9), notice that our sins are not only forgiven but we must accept cleansing; the cleansing of the conscience. No matter how often we appeal to this promise, God does not become weary of forgiving us and cleansing us.

No one *has* to masturbate. Because the sex drive is so powerful, we are tempted to let our passions lie to us; we all admit that our human tendency is to avoid the suffering that comes with temptation. We are programmed to take the path of least resistance, but there are alternatives that help reduce the frequency of this sexual practice, if not eliminate it altogether. The interval between times can become greater, and God stands by to help and to forgive.

## GETTING A PROPER PERSPECTIVE

In fact, masturbation is often practiced in conjunction with pornography, an evil industry that is bent on capitalizing on self-gratification and addictive behavior. With the internet and smart phones which are instantly addictive, young people's hearts today are often captured by the lure of our satanically inspired sexualized culture.

Many Christians are disappointed when God doesn't immediately answer their prayers to be freed from these practices. But sometimes they're praying for the wrong answer: They're expecting God to take away their sexual desires. God usually won't take away our desires but instead gives us grace to resist them. The desires themselves are God-given, though if we give in to them frequently, they may become more intense. God wants to teach us how to overcome temptation rather than remove the temptation completely by neutralizing our sex drive.

Sexual sin of whatever kind, is best overcome with humility and meeting with other believers to pray, seek God, and discuss lessons learned in the midst of struggles, failures, and many victories. We must even thank God for temptations (notice I didn't say that we give thanks for sin). Like one man said, "I told God I would thank Him even if I was tempted until the day I died." Such a life of thanksgiving will help us view our struggle with objectivity and perspective. A person who struggles with masturbation is often so preoccupied with their struggle they can't view themselves objectively. A life of praise helps us stand back and realize God has a purpose in all things.

If you are struggling with masturbation, I suggest that overcoming it should *not* be your highest priority. If so, you will be devastated if you fail. Instead, determine that your goal in life is to become an intimate worshiper of God. Notice that this goal is universal for all Christians, those are married, those who are single and wish to be married, those who are life-long singles, and those who struggle with same-sex attraction. This will help give a proper focus to your life. If you seek first the kingdom of God and His righteousness, victory will eventually be added to you (see Matthew 6:33). To be a Spirit-filled Christian is your ultimate goal. If, in the process, God grants you complete victory over this temptation, fine. Yet if you struggle with it, don't let it deter you from your desire to know God better. And, let us cleave to the promise, "But I say, walk by the Spirit, and you will not gratify the desires of the flesh" (Galatians 5:16).

On a given day you may feel no lust and believe you finally have overcome your temptation. But then suddenly you find yourself burning with desire. Later, you may be surprised and wonder how this could have happened. Of course, we can never assume that any habit which once controlled us has vanished for good. So, it's particularly important to surrender to God every day, whether or not we think we'll be tempted.

What if you lack the desire to stop? Maybe you think you deserve this secret pleasure, and besides, you think you could never overcome it anyway. Mary V. Stewart told about her struggle, "I eventually stopped—again, not without struggle and stumbling, but I stopped. I wanted God's Spirit more than I wanted transient physical titillation, and over and above that, I began to see that abstinence made sense in terms of optimal preparation for *real* sharing with a *real* person."[32] In fact, unmet longings as a single or married person, can point us toward our ultimate satisfaction in the presence of God.

Of course God is patient, for He knows that sexuality is rooted in our very being. He may be working on us in other areas, bringing our life in line so that we continue to grow even though we are struggling. But eventually He will close in; He will patiently prod us to give up the idols of the heart. Best of all, you will be motivated to face the underlying issues that may have contributed to your decision to resign in defeat. But you will not be released from this habit as long as you look within, trying to find out whether you're victorious. Within the human heart is every evil desire; the potential of sin is always with us. It's faith in the Lord Jesus Christ; we must look beyond ourselves to what He has done in our behalf that should be our greatest desire. Our aim is to please Christ, not ourselves.

Let me suggest some basic steps to help overcome temptation:

1. Confess and forsake any sin that may be the cause of your temptation. Pornography, sensual shows or movies, or any other stimulants should be avoided. Earlier I quoted 1 John 1:9 that teaches if we confess our sins God forgives and cleanses us. But—and this is important—to confess means to agree with God; we agree with Him about everything; we agree that He has the right to take the sin out of our hearts forever. We must be totally honest with God and obedient in all he asks us to do.

To speak plainly: God desires deep and abiding repentance. Too many Christians who have a passport in the Heavenly Kingdom, retain their earthly passport, and they move freely between the two. We must have protective barriers between us and the ever-present temptations of the world.

Remember, this will not put an end to the temptation itself, for sin arises within us. As James wrote, "But each person is tempted when he is lured and enticed by his own desire" (James 1:14). But even so, we must control many of the outer stimulants.

2. You must accept yourself and your circumstances. If you are single, thank God for that, even though you may desire marriage. If you're upset with God because He

hasn't given you a partner, you will likely never overcome your temptation. It's this feeling of "I deserve this pleasure because I've been short-changed" that causes a person to give up in the struggle. God has a right to do as He wishes with His own, and unless we accept that, we will fail in our struggle against sin.

Satan's desire is to make us unhappy with our lot in life. Someone has said that marriage is like the flies on a screen door: Those that are out want in, and those that are in want out! At any rate, few people are satisfied. God wants us to be content even when we have unsatisfied desires. God has to teach us that there's more in life than sexual fulfillment. And our love for God must be greater than our love of self.

Remember the story of the potter and the clay? Paul wrote that the clay does not have the authority to tell the potter what to do (Romans 9:21). The clay must submit to the potter, accepting whatever decisions the potter makes on its behalf. When we can accept God's will for us, and particularly distressing circumstances, as from His hand, we'll be in a better position to say *no* to temptation and *yes* to Him.

3. Believe that God through Christ has won a victory over sinful passions. That's tough to believe because people ask, "If that's so, why am I still driven by these desires?" This will be the greatest test of your faith: Will you believe your passions or will you believe God? I'm not implying

that victory is automatic—simply that the foundation for our victory has been laid in Christ.

We all have to learn that when we aren't walking in personal victory, our faith vanishes. Of course it takes time to build faith. Paul prayed that "having the eyes of your hearts enlightened, that you may know what is the hope to which he has called you, what are the riches of his glorious inheritance in the saints" (Ephesians 1:18). Memorizing Romans chapters 6 to 8 will help us engraft the Word of God into our lives and build faith.

For those who find themselves driven by masturbation, perhaps practicing it several times a day, there may have to be a renunciation of satanic powers. Demonic spirits capitalize on our weaknesses, inflaming the passions. This can be done by submission to God and then in faith we say, "Begone, Satan, for it is written," then quote verses of Scripture that assure you of your position in Christ. James has given us this promise, "Submit yourselves therefore to God. Resist the devil, and he will flee from you" (James 4:7).

4. Remember, the easiest time to resist temptation is the moment the fantasies crop up in the mind. That's when the decision is to be made, because it will never get any easier. As the thoughts continue to fester in the mind and the passions are aroused, then masturbation may become inevitable. It's developing sensitivity to the Holy Spirit

that helps us. Yes, there will be failures in the struggle. But God also understands that we are sexual creatures, and He knows how intense the battle can become. So we must be secure in His acceptance of us and know that even when we as believers sin, we are still accepted in the Beloved One.

Begin now to develop habits that will lead you to a fully committed life. God stays with you each step of the way.

## STUDY AND APPLICATION

1. Develop the habit of getting out of bed in the morning when you awaken. Or else recite Scripture and pray, thanking God for the night's rest. To lie in bed with random thoughts is to invite lusts that appear to be under your control, but may soon be beyond your control.

Then spend time with God. Submit yourself to Him fully. Spend time in praise and worship, and ask God to show you those matters in your life that you may be withholding from Him. Spend enough time so that you know your new day is in the hands of God.

2. Memorize such verses as Ephesians 1:22; 2:4–6; 3:20–21. The Word of God cleanses the mind and gives the confidence to face temptation (John 15:3).

3. Choose beforehand how you will respond to sexual thoughts. Quote verses (Matthew 5:8, for example) five times consecutively. This doesn't guarantee you will resist temptation, but if you are submitted to the authority of

the Word, you'll be able to exercise authority over your thoughts and actions.

4. Before you go to bed at night, ask God to cleanse your mind and protect it from any kind of evil thoughts.

5. When you fail, claim instant forgiveness. Don't delay even an hour. God does not find it difficult to forgive you. You may find it difficult to come to Him simply because you are so disappointed in yourself. God forgives completely; He never says, "Oh, no, not *you* again!" Even our constant need of confession is used by God to teach us the wonder of His grace.

CHAPTER EIGHT
# MY FRIEND, THE HOMOSEXUAL

The issue of homosexuality must be included in any discussion of sexuality. There used to be a time when the matter could be dismissed on the grounds (probably mistaken) that only a few people exhibited sexual desire toward their own sex. Today, it's different. Many people, including genuine Christians, find themselves driven by passions over which they seemingly have no control.

Derogatory language in popular culture only contributes to deepening the wedge between homosexuals and heterosexuals. And with the transgender movement, we have an ever-expanding list of sexual issues that must be treated with understanding, compassion, and most importantly, with truth. This chapter, however, is limited to the subject of homosexuality.

A good discussion usually begins with good definitions. The difficulty of speaking to this issue in our current cultural moment is that language is still changing, and terms are still being defined, and then redefined. For this chapter I will most often use the terms homosexual, same-sex attraction, or LGBTQ+ to refer to the attraction to the same sex. Note that just because someone is attracted to the same sex, it doesn't mean they are currently engaging in same-sex sexual activity. In fact, many faithful Christians who are same-sex attracted are exercising costly obedience by refraining from such activity. I will do my best to be clear when I am specifically talking about attraction, and when I am talking about engaging in sinful, sexual activity. Just because I use these terms in this way, I realize that there are those who define these matters differently. If you find yourself in a discussion on this issue, I encourage you to make an effort to understand how these various terms are being used by the person you are talking to.

Even though many Christians may know or know of a person with same-sex attraction, they do not always realize some within the Christian church may be afraid to reveal their struggle with sexual attraction. Sometimes these people are stereotyped even though we can't always recognize them by the way they dress or speak. Some churches may not allow a space for someone to share that they are struggling in this area of their life.

We have also been guilty of misunderstanding the depths of feeling same-sex attracted people may be experiencing. Superficial comments such as "Why doesn't he get married?" are hurtful because they reveal a shallow understanding of what a person thinks and feels. Meeting and counseling those who struggle with same-sex attraction dispels these misunderstandings. If we would take time to understand the pain and sense of rejection these people often endure, we would be more sympathetic. They have the same need for love and respect as anyone. We, the church, need to be their safety net, helping them navigate their sexual struggles.

Imagine yourself in their position: You are a male, 18 years of age. You have a powerful erotic attraction to men. You have not consciously chosen this attraction. Your friends might be attracted to girls, but you are not. The pressure of society and your feelings remind you that you are "abnormal." You try to change, but you can't. You implore God for help, but your passions continue unabated.

What would you do?

Tell your parents? They might not understand. In fact, one organization established decades ago to help the parents of homosexual children is called the Spatula Club— because parents needed to be scraped off the ceiling when they heard the news of their child's same-sex attraction! Tell your pastor? Not if he's the kind who berates homosexuals from the pulpit. You have no idea what he may say to you.

As a result, the common response for the LGBTQ+ individual is to find others with whom they can identify.

They will probably seek acceptance among those who share their viewpoint. If they're a Christian, they might seek to defend themselves, even to the point of reinterpreting the Bible to make their sexual activity acceptable to God and others. If they're not a Christian, they may seek their identity with radical organizations which are intent on changing laws to make LGBTQ+ relationships as respectable as heterosexuality. Some of these radical LGBTQ+ groups believe every school should have a practicing LGBTQ+ person as a teacher so children can grow up viewing these alternative lifestyles as acceptable.

Just consider the disputes between parents and teachers in the past few years and you will know how important it is for parents to be involved in their children's education. Let me say it with clarity: Parents, God will hold you accountable for the education of your children, and you dare not subject them to teachers who believe that abnormal behaviors are normal and that sex should not be limited to a covenantal one man one woman relationship.

Be that as it may, we must be reminded that many who struggle with same-sex attraction have been driven more deeply into that lifestyle because of the insensitivity of the church. They are bitter because they feel Christians don't take time to understand them. Consequently, some have written off the church and have sought their identity elsewhere.

No one should speak about an LGBTQ+ person

without a caring heart. I doubt whether anyone has ever changed by simply hearing a sermon against such lifestyles. The teaching of Scripture must be accompanied with understanding, patience, and love. David Augsburger has wisely said, "It's so much easier to tell a fellowman what to do about his hurts than to stand with him in his pain."[33]

This doesn't mean we reinterpret the Bible to suit the contemporary mindset. I'm not under the illusion the radical gay community will listen, but the church must reach out to Christians with same sex-attraction or anyone in the LGBTQ+ community who is looking for a word of hope, understanding, and compassion. We must try to understand LGBTQ+ individuals and listen to what they say, and feel the pain of rejection they experience before we comment on their lifestyle. We should not seek to be an affirming church (a church that supports LGBTQ+ relationships), but we should seek to be a welcoming church that invites everyone to know Jesus and understand God's plan for human sexuality.

## WHAT DOES THE BIBLE SAY?

The Scriptures teach that homosexual activity is sin. In the Old Testament, more than a dozen of offenses were punishable by death. Among them were adultery and same-sex activity. Specifically, God says, "If a man lies with a male as with a woman, both of them have committed an abomination; they shall surely be put to death; their blood is upon them" (Leviticus 20:13). Now most sins requiring capital punishment could be satisfied with a ransom, but the point still remains that this particular sin is taken very seriously by God.

In Romans 1:26–27 we read that homosexuality is against nature. This means that the homosexual is fighting against the nature of his own body. This is confirmed by Paul's use of the words *exchanged* and *gave up*. It means the homosexual person has abandoned what their body naturally craves. Associated with this are guilt and fear which often drive the person to pursue further homosexual relationships. When Paul says that "God gave them up" it means that God delivers a person over to sin by intensifying the guilt and obsessions in the individual's life. At this point, the person will either come to complete repentance, or they will be driven more intensely by their passions. Paul speaks of the homosexual as "burned in his own lusts" (KJV). This describes the consuming fire of homosexual passion.

The Bible is consistently clear: Both homosexual acts and lusts come under the condemnation of God. It is a distortion of God's will for humanity. Just like a kleptomaniac who told me that he was born a kleptomaniac, and therefore not responsible for his desire to steal, so some practicing homosexuals justify themselves by saying they were born that way. But God holds us responsible for our sinful desires.

I'm not denying that an LGBTQ+ lifestyle may be an unconscious adaptive step taken as a child, but even when this is the case, we can make choices which change our behavior. Ruth Barnhouse, a Christian psychotherapist wrote, "The process of psychotherapy entails a very large element of helping the sufferer to understand that he is not a victim of something beyond himself, but that choices made in the past, however unconsciously, can be reviewed and new decisions taken."[34]

LGBTQ+ desires cannot be excused because some grow up with them and they are therefore "natural." I know of no substantial evidence that says same-sex attraction is communicated genetically, but even if there is inborn predisposition toward particular temptations, that does not remove God's call to holy living. We are all born with "the sin gene" and yet we are accountable for our actions.

There is some evidence that environmental factors, usually coupled with specific experiences, can make a child vulnerable to the redirection of sexual passions. In their excellent book, *Homosexuality—The Use of Scientific Research in the Church's Moral Debate*, Stanton L. Jones and Mark A. Yarhouse discuss many of the arguments put forward by the gay community and show them to be flawed.[35]

## WHAT CAUSES HOMOSEXUALITY?

We must resist the tendency to think that every LGBTQ+ individual fits into a neat stereotype, but there is no doubt that some general patterns emerge when we try to identify the cause of their sexual desires.

Number one there is the family. Mary Stewart Van Leeuwen, a Christian feminist, observes, "It may well be that, irony of ironies, in promoting gay households we may be promoting misogyny...People who are gay-positive tend to think that whatever is good for gays is automatically good for people who care about justice for women." She acknowledges that the "gender injustice" of fatherlessness is already a problem in today's' society without gay marriage, but added, "I don't think we should add to the possibility of more of it."[36] She predicts unforeseen consequences to such a radical overhaul of marriage and family.

Some same-sex attracted individuals grew up in good Christian families with good, loving parents. But many of those in the LGBTQ+ community, had some adverse family dynamics. Many same-sex attracted men and women did not have a good male role model; consequently, their own sexual identity became confused and they simply couldn't relate meaningfully to the opposite sex. Often a passive or absentee father accompanies an over-protective, dominant mother in the home. The boy thus identifies with his mother and assumes her sexual role. One man told me, "My mother dressed me in girls' clothes. At school the kids said, 'He must be queer.' I thought that they must be right, and I began to think about my identity. Soon I was attracted to other males."

If a mother hates men and communicates this to her son, she may make the boy vulnerable to homosexual temptations. Particularly in the absence of a man in the home, the boy might begin to shrink from the male role he should identify with. No one can calculate the amount of damage that hostility between parents contributes to the confusion of sex roles.

Many years ago I was invited to a conference specifically intended to help those who struggled with same-sex attraction and sought to come out of the lifestyle. Over breakfast I found myself sitting at a table with five or six women who struggled with same-sex attraction and I asked them, "If you feel comfortable, would you tell me your story as to how you got into this lifestyle?" Each told a painful story of sexual abuse from a father, a babysitter, a brother, a boyfriend, etc. I left that morning vowing to myself that I would always look upon these dear people with compassion, understanding, and brokenness. Judging is easy; walking with people through their pain is much more difficult. Unresolved emotional wounds leave scars for life.

Almost all children are, at some time, sexually stimulated

by the same sex. For most, it's a fleeting experience. But if those feelings are exploited, they may persist and develop into a sexually promiscuous lifestyle. Psychologists tell us that during puberty, a child is particularly impressionable, and if he or she begins to focus on the same sex, those desires are intensified. Understandably, LGBTQ+ pornography can further inflame those desires.

A child can also be introduced to homosexuality by an older man or woman who desires the child for sexual relationships. This may cause the child to withdraw from normal relationships, and feelings toward the same sex will then intensify. Many who have had such an experience mistakenly believe they are doomed to grow up that way. What began as a one-time experience, ends up becoming a fixed pattern of thought and behavior. Rabbi Akiba is quoted as saying, "At the beginning (sin) is like a thread of a spider's web, but in the end it becomes like a ship's cable."

The final judgment of God on Israel was the scattering of families (see Deuteronomy 28:32, 64). The emotional consequences of divorce on children are much more severe than a natural disaster could ever be. Little wonder God's last Old Testament word to humanity regarding the coming of John the Baptist (Matthew 17:13) included these words, "And he will turn the hearts of fathers to their children and the hearts of children to their fathers, lest I come and strike the land with a decree of utter destruction" (Malachi 4:6).

With the breakup of our homes and harsh and unloving attitudes of parents toward each other and their children, it is not surprising that we have so many who feel the pangs of rejection and hurt. As a result, we have those who are driven by their inner torment to sinful relationships in an attempt to soothe the anxiety, fear, and bitterness latent in their hearts. This explains why an increasing number of people are identifying as part of the LGBTQ+ community. I've written more extensively about this in my book, *The Truth About Same-Sex Marriage.*

Whether they realize it or not, LGBTQ+ people are hurting people. They've been so deeply wounded that they're more aware of the attitudes and feelings of others. They often disassociate themselves from Christians for fear of being rejected again. Unfortunately, this sometimes means they're quick to take up an offense and to harbor bitterness.

For those who admit their need, we ought to provide support and encouragement. Who among us has never been bound by sin which was brought on by the failures of those who have influenced us the most?

## IS THERE A WAY FORWARD?

Christians are divided on whether or not Christ actually changes the desires of those who struggle with same-sex attraction. Because many revert to same-sex relationships after extensive counseling, some feel we should have a less ambitious goal. The most we can expect, they say, is to teach them to resist acting out on their desires. Once an alcoholic, always an alcoholic; once a homosexual, always a homosexual in basic preference, they say. The sexual appetite never changes, and since all of us must say *no* to lust, it really doesn't matter whether our lust is homosexual or heterosexual. In either case, the same biblical teaching applies: "Let not sin therefore reign in your mortal body, to make you obey its passions" (Romans 6:12).

Though such an approach may be laudable, I believe God may take a person *beyond* that to an actual redirection of his or her sexual desires. When Paul discussed various kinds of sinners, he included homosexuals, "And such were some of you. But you were washed, you were sanctified, you were justified in the name of the Lord Jesus Christ and by the Spirit of our God" (see 1 Corinthians 6:9–11). He assumed that Christ had *delivered* these people from their pre-conversion lifestyles.

Of course it's not easy. The Christian who struggles with same-sex attraction should not think that God doesn't love them, nor should they conclude that they can't grow in their faith even while they struggle. I have met those who have displayed the fruit of the Spirit even while they have regarded their condition with sorrow and contrition, but are yet unable to change. They are fellow pilgrims en route to the heavenly city.

With care, I would like to suggest for  some basic processes for Christians who struggle with same-sex attraction, each of which takes time. One step may blend into another or need to be repeated, but I believe Christ is able to deliver from *homosexual actions and lustful desires.*

*Repent of sin without any self-justification.*

I don't think any of us are fully repentant *until we realize we are held responsible for our inability to obey God.* God holds us responsible even though we are, by nature, children of wrath. Grace is never poured out until we come to the point of full contrition and humility.

David learned, "The sacrifices of God are a broken spirit; a broken and contrite heart, O God, you will not despise" (Psalm 51:17). There can be no excuses, no appeals to our genes or our environment. We must take full responsibility for every attitude and every choice. The practicing LGBTQ+ person must renounce their sexual activity, just as a drunkard or an idolater must renounce theirs.

*Uncover hidden bitterness.* Some same-sex attracted individuals have deep-seated fear and bitterness toward members of the opposite sex. Even when they won't admit these feelings, further probing usually reveals unloving attitudes (if not outright bitterness) toward a member of the opposite sex, either within or outside of the family.

There may be even deeper bitterness toward those who have wronged them. Since LGBTQ+ tendencies often grow in ruptured family relationships, it's easy to see why such feelings may be deep-seated and difficult to uncover. Sometimes, they go back to infancy. Those who wish to study one counselor's experience in helping homosexuals to probe beneath the surface of their feelings may want to read *The Broken Image* by Leanne Payne (Crossway Books).

*Find a support person or group.* One Christian girl struggling with same-sex attraction wrote, "Good listening ears were few and far between. I desperately needed people who would listen to me—for hours on end at times. I didn't want pat answers. They were usually much too simplistic or naïve to be helpful. I needed someone who would listen with God's patience and compassion."

We all need a fellow believer with whom we have acceptance. In fact, habits can only be broken when we are accountable for our actions. Without friendship and accountability, there can be no deliverance. For further reading, I highly recommend books by Rosaria Butterfield who came out of a lesbian lifestyle due to the love and hospitality of a pastor and his wife. Her books, including how she became a Christian, are strongly biblical and deeply personal. You may find more information and her books on her website: RosariaButterfield.com.

*Don't become discouraged.* Remember, all of us struggle

with something. We are learning to tear down the strongholds of sin through meditation on Scripture and through full acknowledgement of our sin. Meanwhile, any believer who walks in submission can be a blessing and a testimony to others. We must depend on God's grace even during temptations.

*Remember that God does not reject us as persons.* All who have savingly believed on Christ, can be assured of God's continued love despite struggles with sexual identity and desires. In fact, our core identity becomes a "child of God." God looks on us with the same favor He has for Jesus. Those who struggle with regret and self-hatred find it difficult to accept the idea that God loves us. It's important not to blame God, but to put aside bitterness. As long as we call His goodness into question, we are defeated.

One Christian who struggles with same-sex attraction explained his course of action to me. He learned to look to God and praise Him when temptations came.

Submission to God is the key. When we do this, we will be willing to accept whatever struggles we may have without the bitterness that intensifies them.

*Finally, there must be a renewing of the mind.* This happens only by learning the principles of spiritual warfare. We've got to know who we are in Christ before we can, with confidence, say *no* to temptation. Here is prayer we can all pray:

"Lord when I have the temptation to act out my desires may I not have the opportunity; and when I have the opportunity may it be when I don't have the desire. Keep me from evil at any cost."

Finally, if you are a Christian struggling with same-sex attraction, don't think of yourself as homosexual, for that is not your real identity. Think of yourself as a Christian who struggles with same-sex attraction. For further reading on the biblical basis for our identity in Christ, I recommend *Holy Sexuality and the Gospel* by Christopher Yuan, an agnostic gay man who converted to Christ and now finds his identity in Christ. As I've already emphasized, we all struggle with something. But we await the heavenly city with hope.

## STUDY AND APPLICATION

1. Paul said that those who were formerly homosexuals were now washed, sanctified, and justified (1 Corinthians 6:11). Study these three words and state how they can be applied to our situation today.

2. Paul says all of us are "by nature children of wrath" (Ephesians 2:3). Since we are all accountable for our corrupt natures, does this imply we are responsible even for that over which we have no control? How does this apply to those who have had LGBTQ+ tendencies since puberty?

3. Those who engage in LGBTQ+ activity receive "in

themselves the due penalty for their error" (Romans 1:27). What do you think that penalty might be?

4. Read Philippians 4:4–9. What hints does Paul give about how to think pure and good thoughts rather than evil ones?

CHAPTER NINE
# THE FIRST STEP TO FREEDOM

"Tell me man to man: Is there a way out or isn't there? If there is, I want to know about it; if there isn't, I'm going to blow my brains out."

This was the cry of a desperate man caught in the vice of sexual sin. He was a practicing homosexual, overwhelmed with a sense of guilt, tired of his secret liaisons, weary of making promises that he couldn't keep.

Where does he begin? Precisely where all of us must begin. We must understand that we can be forgiven and have a new beginning. We must settle our past before we can get on with our future, because the sin that condemns us is our master. If we feel guilty and polluted, and are filled with self-hatred, we are doomed to continue as a slave of sin.

Can you identify with what William Justice has written?

For every failure to live up to some *ought*, there is the tendency to punish one's self in such a manner as to produce another failure! And every failure

produces the response, I ought not to have failed!...
Having failed, I punish myself in such a manner
as to produce a further sense of failure. My cycle is
complete only to begin again. I have failed to live up
to an *ought* for which I feel guilty. Convicted of guilt
I feel the need to pay. To pay, I choose a method that
will leave me with a sense of having failed...on and
on rolls the cycle downward. It may be compared
to a snowball rolling downhill, adding to its load
and momentum with each revolution. The load of
guilt that is picked up becomes greater and greater
and the rate of descent becomes faster and faster.
This cycle of the damned goes round and round and
down and down and has the potential of going on
and on eternally. That is at least one aspect of hell.[37]

Time does not obliterate the guilt. Guilt is not simply a
feeling to unlearn. It's not the result of a repressive society. It is
our God-given response to moral failure. No escape through
drugs, sex, or diversionary pleasure can erase its pollution.
Unless we are forgiven and cleansed, we'll give up and say,
"I've already messed up, why shouldn't I do it again?"

Fortunately, God has an excellent remedy for guilt—
forgiveness of sin because Christ, in His death, atoned for
our sins.

An atheist asked Billy Graham, "If Adolf Hitler, on

his deathbed, had received Christ, would he have gone to heaven, whereas someone who lived a good life but rejected Christ would go to hell?" That is a trick question. It was asked to make the gospel appear ridiculous. But the answer is *yes*. If Hitler trusted Christ, God could forgive him completely because Christ's death included all of Hitler's sins! God values Christ so much that He can accept Hitler if he comes to God on the basis of Christ's merit, but He cannot accept a good man without Christ's merit!

In Zechariah 3 we read that Joshua, the high priest, was being cleansed by Jehovah while Satan watched, making accusations. Why was Satan so interested in Joshua's sin? It wasn't because he was concerned about Joshua entering heaven with filthy garments. Satan was angry that God was able to clothe a sinner with clean robes. Satan wanted Joshua to stay in his polluted clothes.

Christ is able to cleanse us despite the protests of the devil and our polluted consciences. Charles Spurgeon wrote:

> Stand where you are; for remember, you are standing in the only place where pollution can be washed away, you are standing before the angel of the covenant. It is before Christ that sin is to be confessed. Confess it anywhere else, your sorrow is not repentance but remorse. "What is remorse?" says one. Remorse is repentance made out of sight of Jesus; true repentance is sorrow of sin in the

presence of Christ. Foul and filthy as you are, there is but one voice which can speak you clean. Go not away from that voice. There is but one hand which can touch you and make you pure; stand where that hand is close to you, and still, filthy as your garments are, shun not the face of your best, your only friend, but breathe out this prayer, "Lord, if Thou wilt, Thou canst make me clean. Purge me, O purge me now, for Thy love's sake."[38]

Have you ever wondered whether your forgiveness is complete? Or maybe you've doubted whether you have genuinely repented? Repentance is not merely a change of mind (as many believe). It is also a change of *direction*. The Scripture is very clear, "If we confess our sins, he is faithful and just to forgive us our sins and to cleanse us from all unrighteousness" (1 John 1:9).

## CONFESSION GOES WITH REPENTANCE

As I have already indicated, the word *confess* literally means "to agree together with." Confession must be combined with repentance. Both words indicate a wholehearted submission to God along with an admission of the evil of sin. To use grace as an excuse for our behavior falls short of full agreement.

A Christian medical student decided to give his

wife an abortion. He knew it was sin, and prayed before the operation, "O God, forgive the sin I am about to commit and guide my hand." Unfortunately, his wife died of complications that came as a result of the surgery. Obviously, his request for forgiveness before he committed his sin was half-hearted repentance. King Saul who died in rebellion against God, repented five times in his lifetime. But half-hearted repentance is not repentance at all. True repentance is not just feeling sorry that we've been caught; true repentance means that we grieve over our sin because we know we have grieved God.

Psalm 51 is an example of true confession. David had to remind himself of the compassionate attributes of God or he might never have come for pardon and cleansing. He began by saying, "Have mercy on me" (v. 1). The Hebrew word for "mercy" means "to give undeserved favor." He was asking for a gift he didn't deserve. David appealed to God's steadfast love, His "unfailing love" (v. 1, NIV). The phrase *steadfast love*, also translated as *lovingkindness* has the same root as the word *stork*, the large bird which builds its nest high in treetops and which is known for its unfailing loyalty to its young (that's why the stork is associated with the birth of a baby). Then he mentions God's great compassion. David was thinking of the compassion a mother has for her helpless baby who can do nothing to care for itself. She doesn't abandon her child but takes delight in caring for them.

God has emotions and can be touched by our feelings of helplessness and of failure. He doesn't turn His back on us. Rather we turn our backs on Him. We don't have to persuade Him to accept us; we need only turn toward him to receive His grace.

We can sense the completeness of David's submission. He's not asking God to help him work himself out of a mess. David leaves it all up to God and is satisfied with whatever God does. A fully repentant person does not come to God with an agenda. There's no attempt to bribe God or to make heroic promises to do better next time. Self-justification gives way to self-abhorrence.

Job spent many hours complaining about God's treatment of him. But when he finally saw God, he forgot his well-rehearsed speeches. "I had heard of you by the hearing of the ear, but now my eye sees you; therefore I despise myself, and repent in dust and ashes" (Job 42:5–6).

As long as we cling to some particle of goodness in ourselves, we have not fully repented. If there are thoughts about keeping our options open—if we think we just might want to sin again—we have not come to full agreement.

The price is further bondage.

## ADMITTING REBELLION AGAINST GOD

We go to great lengths to cover our sin. One man in love with another man's wife kept a device on his telephone to detect whether or not his phone was being tapped. We use lies, deceptions, and playacting to keep sin hidden. We want to hide our sin; God wants to expose it.

What a delusion to believe that even if we think we can keep our sin hidden from others, we can also keep it hidden from God. But our sin is against an omniscient God, the supreme Lawgiver. David uses three words to refer to his immorality—*transgressions, iniquity, and sin*. All of these imply an absolute standard. He had sinned with a clenched fist.

David underscored his rebellion, "Against you, you only, have I sinned and done what is evil in your sight" (Psalm 51:4). We're tempted to say, "Wait a moment, David. You sinned against Bathsheba and you killed Uriah—that wasn't exactly a private act between you and God." But David saw that sin is, first of all, against God. In the process, we hurt others, but sin is first and foremost against the Lawgiver. If a child disobeys his parents who tell him not to touch the vase on the mantle, yet he disobeys and the ornament crashes to the floor, then his baby brother steps on the broken glass, disobedience to his parents is still the basic issue. Whether his baby brother was hurt is secondary.

If Bathsheba had not become pregnant, David would not have killed Uriah, but his relationship with God still would have been ruptured. Whether or not the consequences of sin become evident to others makes little difference to

God. When we sin, we should always remember that our sin is against God, no matter the sin and no matter who else may be involved.

A Christian couple who had premarital sex were disturbed when they thought the woman was pregnant. Their agony was relieved when a physician told her she wasn't pregnant after all, and the couple went to an exclusive restaurant in Chicago for an evening of celebration. They were elated that their fears were groundless. They feared the consequences of their sin, but had no fear of God. A girl who gets an abortion may feel guilty because of what she did to the unborn baby, yet oblivious to what she has done to God.

I can't say it too often, "All are naked and exposed to the eyes of him to whom we must give account" (Hebrews 4:13). Things that are done in secret are going to be proclaimed from the housetop. Shame will no longer be hidden. In heaven, secret sins are already public. To paraphrase Dr. Lewis Sperry Chafer, "A secret sin on Earth is an open scandal in heaven."

A woman in South America brought her dirty laundry to the river. She was so ashamed of her dirty clothes that she didn't want to take them out of the basket in the presence of other women. So she dipped the entire basket of clothes into the water several times and then took them back home. Sometimes that's the way we confess our sins. We admit them to God very quickly and in one big bundle. We are not honest with God or the people around us; we don't take the time to enumerate our sins and how they grieve God.

John White wrote, "We have a choice to make when we come to God about our sin. Either we justify ourselves, or else we justify God. We cannot do both. If I am right, then God is wrong. If I say, 'You would be wrong to condemn me altogether because I cannot really be held responsible,' and so forth, I am challenging the righteous judgments of God. Whether I realize it or not, I am putting God in the wrong."[39]

Are you still softening the full force of your sin? Are you calling adultery "an affair"? Are you pleading that you have certain needs which God ought to take into account? If so, you are not agreeing fully with God.

One man had the habit of looking at pornography. He just looked in order to "keep up with the latest." He'd confess his sins and be restored to fellowship, but a few weeks later, he would be looking again. One day he realized that he didn't really think of what he was doing as sinful. He had been confessing his sins only because he felt guilty, not because he had offended God. When he realized his actions were done in the presence of God and that God might discipline him by letting him become ensnared in sensuality, he developed a healthy fear of his secret practice. "After that," he said, "I never let myself touch it because

I was afraid of what God might bring into my life. I no longer consider it a viable option."

Like a recovered alcoholic who can't afford the risk of one glass of wine, this man finally admitted that pornography was evil and he couldn't trust himself with it. Knowing it was an invitation to slavery, he let God take it out of his life completely. Jesus said, "Sin no more, that nothing worse may happen to you" (John 5:14). Do you see the error of reasoning, "If I sin in a big way, I can be forgiven in a big way, and experience God's grace in a big way"? God might let you be enslaved to a sin in a big way and your heart be hardened in a big way.

## TAKING RESPONSIBILITY FOR SIN

Five times in the first three verses of Psalm 51, David uses the word *me* or *my*. He didn't blame Bathsheba, though she could also have been complicit—what was she doing in the courtyard in full view of David on the rooftop? In his prayer, David continued, said, "Behold, I was brought forth in iniquity, and in sin did my mother conceive me" (v. 5). We are born under the judgment of God.

David didn't use his sinful nature as an excuse. In Philadelphia, someone scribbled on a wall, "Humpty Dumpty was pushed." The message was that nobody is responsible for what he does. It's environment or genes. Not so; we might find our desires are powerful but ultimately

God holds us responsible for our sin.

We're tempted to say God's standards are too high, that He is mocking us by setting up a standard He knows we cannot reach. We must remember that God has reached down to help us. I remind you again of what Augustine said, "Give what You command, and command what You will."[40] Through Christ we can be forgiven and accepted by God.

Agreeing with God means we have no excuses left. We come defenseless into the presence of God with no objection to whatever God wants to do. A.W. Tozer wrote: "God rescues us by breaking us, by shattering our strength and wiping out our resistance. Then He invades our natures with that ancient and eternal life which is from the beginning. So He conquers us and by that benign conquest saves us for Himself."[41]

## ACCEPTING CLEANSING AS WELL AS FORGIVENESS

In a previous chapter, I mentioned the need to accept cleansing as well as forgiveness. David did this. Let us hear him pray, "Wash me thoroughly from my iniquity, and cleanse me from my sin!" (Psalm 51:2). Cleansing is the subjective application of forgiveness. Forgiveness is what God does *outside* of us. Forgiveness has to do with our legal standing in the sight of God; when He forgives us, we are credited with Christ's righteousness. Cleansing is what God does *inside* purifying our minds and consciences.

If we have come to Christ for forgiveness but still feel guilty about a sin in our past, our feelings will catch up to our theology when we insist on cleansing. Once we have confessed a specific instance of sin, we do not have to confess it again. Because of Christ's work on the cross on our behalf, forgiveness and cleansing is ours by faith.

A polluted conscience smothers the joy and gladness that Jesus came to bring us. David knew the problems his sin caused could not be straightened out, yet he could sing for joy. He wanted to be so clean that the stain would be gone forever.

Fresh snow comes down from heaven without any visible impurities. It can be so white it nearly blinds the eye, and yet David prayed that the Lord would make him "whiter than snow." Isn't that gracious of God?

Almost every satanic attack is directed toward our consciences. Evil spirits desire to make us feel foul, dirty, and beyond hope. Such feelings of self-hatred cannot be met by trying to convince ourselves that we are really beautiful people. Rather, we've got to admit there is no good thing within us; we have no inner resources to meet such an attack. By depending on Christ we are washed, and that's where sin's power loses its grip.

Psychiatrists are prescribing drugs to help people

sleep when God might be wanting to keep them awake with a guilty conscience! This is intended to lead them to repentance, cleansing, and rest in God.

## ACCEPT GOD'S DISCIPLINE

A sure way to tell whether a person is fully repentant is their attitude toward discipline. Not one of us likes to have our sins exposed, but if they are, we must accept it without complaint.

The difference between David and Saul is found in their attitudes when they repented. Saul said, "I have sinned; yet honor me now before the elders of my people" (1 Samuel 15:30). That kind of confession can be said a thousand times without attracting the mercy of God.

David also said, "I have sinned," but there was no struggle to maintain his reputation or even his position as king. Later when he was forced to leave Jerusalem, he asked that the ark of God be returned to the city. "If I find favor in the eyes of the LORD, he will bring me back and let me see both it and his dwelling place. But if he says, 'I have no pleasure in you,' behold, here I am, let him do to me what seems good to him" (2 Samuel 15:25–26).

A woman, upset because she was disciplined by the church, complained about the treatment she received. Truth be told, the discipline was done carefully, humbly, and proportionately. Yet, she gossiped about the elders and what they had done. Such an attitude betrays a lack of repentance. A person who is broken because of their sin will submit to discipline, even if they feel it's unjust; it is received as from the Lord. As long as one pleads for special treatment, as long as there are attempts at self-justification, the repentance is incomplete.

I'm not suggesting that all sexual sins be made public, but when we fully agree with God, we no longer attempt to cover our sin. "Whoever conceals his transgressions will not prosper, but he who confesses and forsakes them will obtain mercy" (Proverbs 28:13). A repentant man submits his reputation to God and trusts Him to do "whatever is best in His sight." Richard Roberts wrote that a person is repentant when "fear of exposure and shame so  long dreaded will now be thought as nothing in comparison with the prospect of cleansing and renewal."[42]

Submission to discipline also means agreeing to make restitution. Maybe all we can do is humble ourselves, asking the forgiveness of those we've wronged. Without a spirit of contrition, we are still harboring rebellion in our hearts.  When Christians begin to make restitution, you can be sure that a spirit of revival is at work.

## A CLEAN SLATE

The Old Testament distinguishes two kinds of sins. One is a sin of passion, the kind committed on the spur of the moment. Another is a sin of defiance or "sinning with a high hand." David committed both kinds of sin. It took Uriah four days to come to Jerusalem, and he was in Jerusalem three days before he went back to the battle. David had a long time to think about his plot to kill his loyal soldier. He sinned with a high hand.

Furthermore, adultery and murder were sins for which there was no Old Testament sacrifice. Both were to be punished by stoning. That's why David in his prayer said, "For you will not delight in sacrifice, or I would give it; you will not be pleased with a burnt offering" (Psalm 51:16). There was no restitution for these sins. David could weep night and day, and live with remorse until he died, but Bathsheba's purity would never be restored, nor would Uriah be brought back to life. Yet, David found forgiveness because he cast himself helplessly before a gracious God.

Have you met people who have committed sins for which there is no restitution? I know a Christian man who is tormented knowing that he fathered a child and that somewhere his girlfriend was having to raise that child by herself. He found the grace to tell his wife about his past, because he couldn't live with the knowledge that he was withholding this dark secret from the woman he married. She forgave him, even as he sought to support the child he had fathered. Even in such circumstances, God forgives and cleanses.

Then there is a couple who gave up a child for adoption. After they were converted to Christ, they discovered that their baby had been placed in the home of a couple who belong to a religious cult. They have to live with the thought that their child is not having a Christian upbringing. The past can't be relived; the consequences of our decisions continue, but God grants grace to the repentant.

A man had developed the art of seduction and introduced young women into prostitution. He had fathered a number of children through his liaisons. Can a man like that be forgiven? Imagine trying to manage the guilt on your own; imagine if you simply try to compartmentalize the past and move to a better future. But the past always returns; push a basketball under the water in a lake, and it will pop up in places you never thought. If we attempt to wash ourselves, we will still be filthy; if God washes us, we will be clean.

If we say that God can forgive us but we can't forgive ourselves, that's devilish pride. Do we require more than God? Do we really have a right to withhold forgiveness for ourselves if God Himself, the pure and Holy One, has granted it? Remorse is nothing more than trying to face our sin apart from Christ.

In John 8, we read about a woman who was caught in adultery. The Pharisees wanted Christ to stone her. He replied, "Let him who is without sin among you be the first to throw a stone at her" (v. 7). When they couldn't do so because of their own sins, He turned to her and said, "Neither do I condemn you; go, and from now on sin no more" (v. 11).

Someone has said that God casts our sins into the depths of the sea then puts up a sign which reads "NO FISHING." "The sacrifices of God are a broken spirit; a broken and contrite heart, O God, you will not despise" (Psalm 51:17). These are the first steps to freedom from sensuality.

## STUDY AND APPLICATION

1. A clear example of halfhearted repentance is that of King Saul. Study these passages to find out why Saul fell short of "full agreement" with God. 1 Samuel 15:24–31; 24:16–22; 26:21–25; and 28:6–25.

2. Read Job 40:1–5 and 42:1–6. What did Job have to repent of? What are some of the characteristics of his repentance?

3. Read Daniel's prayer of repentance in Daniel 9:3–19. What additional insights does he add to our understanding of repentance?

4. The book of Judges can be summed up in the cycle of repentance and chastisement in 2:11–23. What were the steps in this cycle? What disciplines did God impose? How does this apply to us?

## CHAPTER TEN

# CHRIST CAN CHANGE US

"Every renewed soul is the scene and stage, wherein the two mightiest contraries in the world, the Spirit and the flesh, that is, light and darkness, life and death, heaven and hell, good and evil, Michael and his angels, and the dragon with his, are perpetually combating hand to hand," said Puritan writer John Gibbon.[43]

We all have been irritated by someone who, in all seriousness, expects us to do the impossible. It's like telling someone who's depressed to "Cheer up!" as if emotions can be turned on or off like a light switch.

The Bible is filled with seemingly impossible commands. "Let not sin therefore reign in your mortal body, to make you obey its passions" (Romans 6:12). Paul wrote as if we can simply say, "Okay, lust—you can do whatever you please, but I'm not going to obey you anymore. No more fantasies, pornography, or masturbation—that's it!"

Who hasn't said, "Never again" to some sin, only to

come back to the point of having to say it again and again.

Is Paul giving us an impossible command? Is God mocking us by giving standards that are beyond us and then berating us for falling short? Mark Twain is said to have expressed anger toward God for giving to each human being a source of joy and pleasure of sex, then forbidding its use until marriage and restricting it to one partner.

Are some of God's commands impossible? Think of the words of Jesus to the man who had been sick for 38 years. He said, "Take up your bed, and walk" (John 5:11). The man might have reasonably replied, "Heal me first, and *then* I'll walk!" But he didn't say that. In faith he obeyed, and God took over from there. The sick man was asked to do the impossible, and to his astonishment, he could!

Paul recognized that this inclination to lust lies in every human heart (Romans 6:12). How can we make sure that sin doesn't *reign* in our mortal body? Enablement comes with the command. Regardless of our excuses and rationalizing, Paul wouldn't command us to turn away from lust unless he thought such freedom was possible for every believer. *Everything God asks us to do is based on what He has already done* to make victory possible for us. Jesus' work on the cross has provided us with forgiveness of sin and a way to the Father, and the Holy Spirit within gives us power for living. God's standard is high, but His power is available to use against lust or any other sin. A thorough understanding of God's provision for us is necessary to fully apply it in our lives.

## UNDERSTANDING THE CROSS

We receive two benefits from Christ's death. We're better acquainted with the first than the second. Do you remember when you realized that forgiveness is not based on good works—that Christ's death made a complete sacrifice to God for sins? Jesus paid my whole debt to God. On the cross Jesus said, "It is finished." That means our debt has been "paid in full."

Have you ever counseled someone who believes salvation is a cooperative effort between man and God? Good works and faith are needed, the argument goes. Such theology breeds uncertainty. We can't be sure our part is enough; and what is more, the Bible teaches that God doesn't accept our righteousness.

Because Christ's work is complete, our responsibility is to believe (see Ephesians 2:8–9). The New Testament teaches Christ not only paid the whole debt, but *He also won the full war.* His provision for us did not end with His sacrifice for us. In Colossians, we are reminded of His continuing work. "Having forgiven us all our trespasses, by canceling the record of debt that stood against us with its legal demands. This he set aside, nailing it to the cross. He disarmed the rulers and authorities and put them to open shame, by triumphing over them in him" (Colossians 2:13b–15).

We must not be misled. Satan is still on the loose and rebellion is rampant. Because people are shaking their fists at God and doing whatever they please, we might get the impression that Christ's victory was not decisive.

The outcome is never in doubt. He is far above all rival powers. God the Father "worked in Christ when he raised him from the dead and seated him at his right hand in the heavenly places, far above all rule and authority and power and dominion, and above every name that is named, not only in this age but also in the one to come. And he put all things under his feet" (Ephesians 1:20–22).

This means angels, demons, and nations. God tolerates rebellion because He has graciously chosen to postpone judgment. He is waiting until the world is on the brink of self-destruction, then He will return to rule as King of kings and Lord of lords. All legal questions of His authority and power are settled; Christ will rule the world. We have to be firmly convinced that Christ is the Mighty Conqueror, to visualize Him seated in heaven, His work finished. The battle is over. He is representing His people before God.

What difference should this make to us who struggle with the two-steps-forward and three-steps-back routine? We know Christ is victorious, but He seems far away from our personal struggles.

The good news is that all believers are personally identified with Christ's victory. More than 100 times Paul refers to us as being "in Christ." We are even seated with Him at the right hand of God the Father (see Ephesians 2:6). We have two addresses: one on Earth, the other in heaven. We have been delivered from the domain of darkness and transferred to the kingdom of His beloved Son (see Colossians 1:13).

If we grasp these facts, we know we don't have to obey our passions. We can participate in Christ's authority over them. If this weren't true, the commands in the New Testament would only mock us; but just as God knows we can't forgive our own sins, He knows we can't free ourselves from their power either. To paraphrase Andrew Murray, "Remember that however much you abhor what is revealed of self within, and however much you long to be delivered from it, no effort on your own, no self-abhorrence or self-crucifixion will bring the slightest relief. It is God who must do it."

Paul repeatedly exhorts us to holiness, not because we can change our character on our own, but because we are "in Christ," we can let God do it, and our position in Christ can affect our practices. And the blessed Holy Spirit is given to us to experience what Christ has done for us.

Read Paul's epistles and you'll be impressed with the number of commands he gives that are firmly rooted in our position in Christ. In Romans, for example, we read of being baptized into Christ, participating in His death and resurrection. Because of what God has done, He can give the command, "So you also must consider yourselves dead to sin and alive to God in Christ Jesus" (Romans 6:11). Or Paul's statement, "If then you have been raised with Christ" becomes the basis for a whole list of commands including, "seek the things that are above, where Christ is, seated at the right hand of God" (Colossians 3:1) and "Put to death therefore what is earthly in you: sexual immorality, impurity, passion, evil desire, and covetousness, which is idolatry" (3:5).

In some cases, Paul spends whole chapters telling us who we are in Christ before he gives specific commands regarding Christian living (see Ephesians chapters 1–3). The reason we can say *no* to the flesh is not because of how we feel, for our feelings fluctuate, nor because we've had a good time with the Lord in devotions this morning, for some mornings we don't. Nor is it because we've been a Christian for 20 years. It's not even because of the depth of our own yieldedness. It's certainly not because we've become tired of failure and resolved to do something about it. That's like thinking an elephant could fly if he really got serious about it. The reason we can obey God's commands is because of what He has already done for us in Jesus Christ, and we learn to look to Him to do what we cannot.

If Christ, who is our Head, is in heaven and we are members of His body, doesn't it follow that we also have access to the Father and "sit" at God's right hand? Sin is under our feet too!

## USING OUR AUTHORITY

I used to ponder Paul's words, "For sin will have no dominion over you, since you are not under law but under grace" (Romans 6:14). I couldn't understand why being under grace means we are free from sin's power. Then I realized that under the Law, we would have to serve God in order to be blessed. Under grace, God blesses me first and then enables me to serve Him. We can obey from a position of strength.

Let me Illustrate this.

In St. Louis, an unmarried woman and an older married man were living together. She felt guilty and angry about the relationship. When a friend suggested she move out, she immediately replied, "I can't do that...I own the apartment!"

She had asked her live-in companion to leave, but he wouldn't budge. He threatened that if she insisted, he'd "get even." They had lived together for more than a year, and he argued that he had a "right" to the apartment, whether they were married or not.

The woman ignored his threats and went to an attorney

to get a court order that he be evicted. He ranted and raved. She even needed police protection because she was so terrified. When he finally left, she had the locks in the apartment changed. And though she's still frightened, she is on her way to spiritual and emotional recovery.

What gave a 115-pound woman the courage to evict a 200-pound man? *The law was on her side.* In the final analysis, the man had no rights, regardless of how loudly he shouted. Just so, all of our legal battles are taken care of; we have a right to evict the enemy (the flesh and the devil) from the premises. These enemies don't leave peacefully. They argue, lie, and threaten. They remind us of all the benefits we'd receive if we'd just continue to serve them. They even make promises to change, but they won't leave. Even when they're forced to go, they try to contact us again to see if we are ready to compromise and welcome them back.

We have the authority to say *no* to the flesh. Our enemies have been defeated. Faith commands them in the name of Jesus to leave, despite their protests. Unless we know who we are and understand our rights, we will say, "I've tried to change but can't." Even yielding ourselves to God, important though that is, won't be of much help unless we are firmly convinced that God enables us to say *no* to our illicit passions. In Christ, we have won the war.

Because Christ had people like us in mind when He

died, His power can be applied to anyone. Our passions may be unusually powerful, but that's no reason why we must be under their authority. It's not a matter of becoming stronger so that we can master them. Strength comes not by resolutions, but by faith in Christ's victory. If we compare our desires to the power of God, we can take heart. There is hope.

When Hudson Taylor learned to depend fully on Christ, he made the startling discovery that it didn't matter where he was or how great his difficulties were. After all, God had to meet Taylor's needs, therefore whether they were great or small was really irrelevant. "It little matters to my servant whether I send him to buy a few cash worth of things, or the most expensive articles. In either case he looks to me for the money and brings me his purchases."[44] We have resources equal to any emergency. Dealing with our passions is not impossible.

Failures may come if we resist Christ's authority. We may do fine for a while, but without continual dependence on Him we will fail.

## UNDERSTANDING THE HOLY SPIRIT

Before we were converted, we may not have sensed any conflict within us. Perhaps we fulfilled our desires as we saw fit. When we trusted Christ as Savior, we received the Holy Spirit. The Spirit confronts the power of the flesh.

Paul speaks of this conflict, "For the desires of the flesh are against the Spirit, and the desires of the Spirit are against the flesh, for these are opposed to each other, to keep you from doing the things you want to do" (Galatians 5:17).

Paul precedes this description of the conflict by an important statement: "But I say, walk by the Spirit, and you will not gratify the desires of the flesh" (5:16). That's a promise we can sink our teeth into. Regardless of how strong our desires may be, they are not as powerful as the Holy Spirit. If we walk in the Spirit, there's no way our passions can rule us.

Paul stressed the need to cooperate with the Holy Spirit in freeing us from the power of the flesh. "For if you live according to the flesh you will die, but if by the Spirit you put to death the deeds of the body, you will live" (Romans 8:13). If then we understand the power of the Holy Spirit, we will resist temptation and be out of the swamp of moral slavery. "But the fruit of the Spirit is love, joy, peace, patience, kindness, goodness, faithfulness, gentleness, self-control; against such things there is no law" (Galatians 5:22–23). There it is: *self-control.*

Many Christians know the Holy Spirit has power, but for them, walking in the Spirit is reserved for missionaries and pastors. The power of the Spirit is beyond the grasp of ordinary Christians. Most of us reason backward. We think that if we could be more victorious over the flesh, God would reward us by giving us the fullness of the Holy Spirit. So we struggle, hoping someday we'll be good enough to experience the Holy Spirit's power. But Paul would say we've got it backward. We are not given the Holy Spirit as a reward for fighting against the flesh, but as a Helper to fight the flesh successfully. A defeated Christian needs the Spirit's power now—not five years down the road. The Spirit indwells every believer and His power is available to every child of God.

How can the Spirit's power be released? There are two basic requirements: First, we're not to grieve the Holy Spirit (Ephesians 4:30). Paul lists a whole catalog of sins that must be confessed so that the Spirit is not hindered in His work. The Holy Spirit is sometimes represented by a dove, a bird that is particularly sensitive and gentle. We must take inventory and ask whether there are sins that have not been "put away."

Second, the Spirit's fullness must be received by faith. Christ invited people to come to Him and drink, "Whoever believes in me, as the Scripture has said, 'Out of his heart will flow rivers of living water.' Now this he said about the Spirit, whom those who believed in him were to receive, for as yet the Spirit had not been given, because Jesus was not yet glorified" (John 7:38–39). The giving of the Spirit depended on the ascension of Christ. Christ's work on the cross is the reason why God can forgive us; His ascension is the reason why the Spirit can fill us.

How can we bring this into our experience? We may feel unworthy of the Spirit's power, or think there will be a more convenient time, but if we have received the forgiveness of the Cross, we can receive the power of the Ascension.

F.B. Meyer, the twentieth-century English evangelist, told of his experience. "I left the prayer meeting and crept away into the lane praying, 'O Lord, if there was ever a man who needs the power of the Holy Spirit, it is I. But I do not know how to receive Him, I am too tired, too worn, too nervously run-down to agonize.' Then a voice said to me, 'As you took forgiveness from the hand of the dying Christ, take the Holy Spirit from the hand of the living Christ.'" Meyer continued. "I took for the first time and have kept on taking ever since."[45]

## THE NEED FOR FAITH

God wants us to believe Him, not our emotions. Sure, Satan influences our feelings, but we must be able to hold on to the truth. The person of faith believes God even in the fluctuating circumstances of life. To quote a well-worn cliché, "Feelings are not facts!"

One of the best illustrations of faith is when the ten lepers came to Jesus for healing. Jesus told them to go to the priest to be pronounced healed. "And as they went they were cleansed" (Luke 17:14, italics added). Although they were not yet healed, they obeyed the command, and only then did the healing take place. Obeying came before the healing.

How can we increase our faith? D.L. Moody said that for many years, he struggled to have strong faith—it eluded him. Then he read, "So faith comes from hearing, and hearing through the word of Christ" (Romans 10:17). He stopped praying for faith and began to spend more time in the Scriptures.

Our faith will increase when we learn to praise God for whatever happens in our lives. He still seeks worshipers (see John 4:24). He is honored by a life of persistent praise and thanksgiving, "The one who offers thanksgiving as his sacrifice glorifies me" (Psalm 50:23).

You will find your love for God increasing while your love for sinful pleasures diminishes. Just as we lose our desire for steak when we nibble on a candy bar, so the pleasures of the world spoil our appetites for God. He wants to give us a desire for Himself—and it happens when we are immersed in His Word. Let us lay hold of God's promises so that the flesh need not reign in our mortal body.

## STUDY AND APPLICATION

1. What do you think Paul meant when he spoke of us being dead with Christ? (Romans 6:1–7).

2. Give an example of how a person might "consider himself to be dead to sin (Romans 6:11).

3. What does it mean to become a "slave of righteousness"? (Romans 6:18).

4. In Romans 8:13 we read, "By the Spirit you put to death the deeds of the body." What is our part in this process?

5. How would you contrast the works of the flesh and the fruit of the Spirit? (Galatians 5:16–26).

6. What practical steps can you take right now to apply to your life the victory that comes from the cross and the Holy Spirit?

CHAPTER ELEVEN

# WE CAN CONTROL OUR THOUGHTS

"Over the past three years my mind has become filthy. Thoughts that never used to enter remain with me now. I am obsessed. In my mind's eye, I see people having sexual relationships. I can't help myself. Though I've prayed about my condition, prayer seems unreal to me; there is no real depth and I find it hard to focus my mind on God. I know God is merciful and I have no intention of frustrating His goodness and long-suffering toward me. My problem is my mind, which seems to be beyond control. What do you think of my condition?"

The above letter came to me from someone who heard a message I preached on the radio about the need for sexual purity. The dissidence between what we know and our experience often does not match; in other words, we know the truth, but living it is another matter. Nowhere is this more true than in the matter of sexuality.

In John Bunyan's classic work *Chronicles of Mansoul*,

the fortress was besieged by strong, malignant forces, but the enemies couldn't take the fortress until its gates were opened from the inside. How would the fortress eventually be captured? Diabolus (the devil) speaking to his cohorts says, "We'll cajole them, delude them, pretending things that will never be and promising things they shall never get. Lies, lies, lies—the only way to get Mansoul to let us in. And so our intentions will be invisible and we will be invisible—that is, all except one of us."[46]

Thus Satan got the human mind to cooperate with him and we've been reaping the consequences ever since. The strategy remains the same—lies, lies, lies.

We all know battles are won or lost in the mind. The most important part of us is that which nobody sees— except God. If we could flash all of the thoughts we had last week on a screen, we'd have a pretty good idea of our spiritual condition. We also know that shame which would drive us to run and hide.

The mind is particularly strategic because it works in conjunction with the brain. Thoughts are not physical, they are essentially spiritual in nature. This means our thoughts are not forced on us either because of the chemistry of the brain or the feelings of the body. Yet, we all know what it's like to be a slave to the mind. Jonathan Edwards would say we have the natural equipment (mind, emotion, and will), but we lack the moral ability to think rightly. Every honest person agrees!

Because the mind is spiritual in nature, it exists in the same realm as God, angels, and demons. Little wonder it is the scene of incredible battles. We have our own lusts to contend with as well as spiritual forces that vie for our allegiance.

Paul wrote, "Do not be conformed to this world, but be transformed by the renewal of your mind, that by testing you may discern what is the will of God, what is good and acceptable and perfect" (Romans 12:2). The key is to be transformed (the Greek word is *metamorphis*) rather than be pushed into the mold of the world. God wants to change our thought patterns so that our lives are conformed to the image of Christ.

Think what we are up against. By nature we have a "reprobate mind" (Romans 1:28, KJV), a "carnal mind" (Romans 8:7, KJV). In fact, Paul writes, "Because the carnal mind is enmity against God: for it is not subject to the law of God, neither indeed can be" (Romans 8:7, KJV). Accepting Christ as Savior gives us a new nature, but often the old thought patterns continue.

And, if we enter the devil's territory, he has access to our minds as seen in the story of Ananias and his wife Sapphira (Acts 5:3). Little wonder Paul describes the mind as a stronghold or fortress, and testifies, "We destroy arguments and every lofty opinion raised against the knowledge of

God, and take every thought captive to obey Christ" (2 Corinthians 10:5).

What an encouragement to know that our stray thoughts can be captured and brought into submission to Christ! The Holy Spirit is then free to work through our minds, to give us freedom from immorality. "To set the mind on the Spirit is life and peace" (Romans 8:6).

We can yield and surrender, beg and plead, but until our minds are renewed, we will always revert to patterns of sinful thought and behavior. God has given us the equipment we need to dismantle the imaginations of the mind in order that we might be free to serve Christ. *Everything God asks us to do is possible because of what Christ has already accomplished.*

How is the mind renewed? There's no formula, but we must build some specifics into our walk with God. If we are consistent, we will find the promises of the New Testament completely reliable.

## WE NEED A WORSHIPFUL MIND

We've got to begin with a proper understanding of God. Remember the adage: The smaller your God, the bigger your problem; the bigger your God, the smaller your problem.

We've learned that God has much at stake in our temptations. He was deeply grieved by David's sin. He had to scrap greater plans for David's future, and His name was blasphemed by the heathen. If we want to think rightly, our first question is: Do I have a heart for God? Too often we want victory as an end in itself, but such freedom should be a step toward Christlikeness which is God's ultimate purpose. Fellowship with God is more important than victory over sin (though we need the latter to enjoy the former). God Himself must be first in our thinking when we talk about freedom from immorality.

Do I want to master my passions just so I can have a clear conscience, live a successful life, and raise a fine family; or am I fully committed to living for the praise of God's glory?

God lets us struggle so that, in the end, we will have a greater appreciation of Him. Too often we run away when we fail, hoping to hide from God as Adam and Eve did in the Garden of Eden. God is calling us even through our shame and our guilt. He's waiting for us to give up our idols and fully surrender our hearts to Him. He sifts us to separate the wheat from the chaff. He tests us to see where our loyalties really lie. When overcome with fierce temptation, which side do we take? Either way, God is the One with whom we have to deal; everything depends on our relationship with Him.

A friend was so weary of lust that he prayed, "God, if I commit adultery I will disgrace your name. Either take these thoughts out of my mind or strike me dead. I don't want to discredit you." At that point God, along with angels and any demons that might have been listening, knew this man was fully submitted to God. That was the beginning of his freedom from unabated sexual cravings. The temptations never left, but he had crossed a line and rejected those thoughts in the name of Jesus.

Are we that jealous of God's honor? Or do we want to be released from the torment of sexual temptation so life will be easier? If we are concerned only about ourselves, we are using God to our own ends. He becomes the means to our own clear consciences and wholesome self-images.

If we love God with mind, heart, and soul, we'll continue to worship Him even if He doesn't free us from our sexual frustrations. We have an obligation to keep that first commandment (Exodus 20:3) whether or not He does what we think He should.

We must ask ourselves the question: When we succumb to temptation, what concerns us the most? Is it the guilt we experience, is it wondering whether anyone will find out, or the fact that we have grieved the Holy Spirit who is God (see Ephesians 4:30).

Fellowship with God is the best deterrent for lust. One man writing anonymously in *Leadership* about his struggle with pornography said that all the negative arguments didn't work for him. The dire warnings about a failing marriage, guilt, or punishment didn't prevent him from visiting strip clubs and looking at porn. Then he read a book by François Mauriac and his attitude changed. Mauriac concluded that there is only one reason to seek purity. "It is the reason Christ proposed in the Beatitudes: 'Blessed are the pure in heart for they shall see God.' Purity is the condition for a higher love— for a possession superior to all possessions: God Himself." The writer continued, "We are the ones who suffer if we sin, by forfeiting the development of character and Christlikeness that would have resulted if we had not sinned....Here was a description of what I was missing by continuing to harbor lust: I was limiting my own intimacy with God."[47]

I think it was George Müller who said, "The foremost duty of every Christian is to have his soul satisfied in his God." Here is the ultimate reason to surrender the control of our passions to God.

How much time are you giving to worshiping God? Is your fellowship with Him growing?

## THINK ABOUT TRUTH

Paul wrote about the Gentiles (the unconverted) as walking in "the futility of their minds. They are darkened in their understanding" (Ephesians 4:17–18). In Psalm 2, the writer asks, "Why do the nations rage and the peoples plot in vain?" (Psalm 2:1).

Modern man is filled with vain imaginations. Sexualized

shows and movies, erotic literature, and the internet have exposed the inner imaginations, while also causing millions to develop powerful fantasies based on lies; namely, that our way is better than God's. This flood of sensuality has ignited discontent and a callous disregard for the rights of others. No one is satisfied, so we are prone to believe lies: A sexy wife would produce greater satisfaction; our own autonomous freedom is more satisfying than being tied down to a family; and a life of ease is ultimate happiness. Responsibility is old-fashioned. Whatever feels best at the moment is what we ought to do.

Some are caught between two worlds: the reality of day-to-day existence, and the lure of the imagination where real happiness (supposedly) exists. The real world becomes dull and boring compared with this world of unbridled imagination. The exhilaration of drugs and alcohol provides an escape from the realities of a humdrum existence. When the tension becomes unbearable, people will abandon everything and take the plunge into a fantasy world. A Christian woman said she had become so hooked on reality television that she decided to have an affair. She thought, *There's a whole world out there that I'm missing.* Families are split, promises broken, and lives fractured—all because of lies.

Samuel Baker tells a story of Egyptian troops who were dying of thirst in the Nubian Desert. In the distance, they saw what they thought was water, but the Arabian guide warned them that it was only a mirage. An argument erupted and the guide was killed. The whole regiment rushed toward the water. Mile after mile the thirsty troops trudged deeper into the desert as the glistening mirage led them on. Finally they realized that the lake they thought was there was nothing but burning sand. They died pursuing an attractive illusion.

Here are some of the lies that many believe today:

- God is unfair in giving us passions and then restricting their fulfillment.
- By careful planning, we can sin secretly without harm.
- An erotic pleasure is worth any discipline which God might impose as a result.
- We can live in the world of fantasy and still be committed Christians.

Once we have firmly rejected these lies, we must get on with meditating on truth. Christ prayed to the Father, "Sanctify them in the truth; your word is truth" (John 17:17). We must meditate on Scripture day and night. God promises, "Blessed is the man who walks not in the counsel of the wicked, nor stands in the way of sinners, nor sits in the seat of scoffers; but his delight is in the law of the LORD, and on his law he meditates day and night" (Psalm 1:1–2).

Let me introduce you to the principle of replacement. Jesus told a story of a man who had been indwelt by a demon. After the wicked spirit was expelled, it passed through waterless places, seeking rest. Finding none, it decided to return to its original abode, and to its satisfaction, saw that its original house was unoccupied, swept, and put in order (see Luke 11:24–26). Though the man had been free for a time, he had not substituted something God-honoring in place of the demon. When the demon returned, it brought seven others that were more evil than itself, and the man was worse off than before.

Let's do an experiment. I want you to think about the number seven; visualize it in your mind for a second or two. Now, I want you to stop thinking of the number seven. Can you do it? Of course not; just thinking about taking that number out of our mind means we are focusing on it!

But now, let us substitute another thought: I want you to think of your mother, whether she is dead or alive; whether she was a mother who cared for you or rejected you—I just want you to think of her. Do that for a second or two and the number seven will vanish from your mind.

Apply that to your scriptural meditation: Want to get rid of worldly thoughts? Substitute God's thoughts through scriptural mediation and memorization.

## FEEDING THE MIND

God has never stopped revealing to His people that our dependence on Him is moment-by-moment. That's why He told the Israelites they weren't to store manna in their tents (except on the day before the Sabbath). The sight of thousands of people kneeling on the ground searching for manna each morning was a reminder that they needed God's blessing *every day*.

Why was God so strict about this? Because He didn't want them to get to the point where they could survive on their own. He was giving them a lesson in dependence. Quite literally, they were between God and the deep Red Sea! They could not let a day go by without waiting on God to feed them.

In the New Testament, Christ is pictured as the manna that came down from heaven, "Truly, truly, I say to you, it was not Moses who gave you the bread from heaven, but my Father gives you the true bread from heaven. For the bread of God is he who comes down from heaven and gives life to the world" (John 6:32–33). Christ invites us to receive spiritual food from Him. We must follow the pattern of getting it daily, as Israel did. Christians go to church assuming they'll receive enough blessing to last all week.

Our lives would be changed if we spent twenty minutes with God each day before nine o'clock in the morning.

Such discipline would keep us spiritually refreshed, and we would begin each day committing ourselves to God.

The greatest difficulty is in getting started. The second is to keep going.

Remember the story of the man who said he had a good dog and a bad dog with him? When someone asked which one was the strongest, he replied, "The one I feed the most."

Some Christians have starved their new nature so much that they have lost their appetite for spiritual reality. It takes a while to get it back.

## BE RUDE TO SINFUL THOUGHTS

Think of your mind as a castle, then determine what thoughts you should admit and which you should expel from the premises. When lust, greed, ungratefulness, and other enemies knock for entry, don't even give them the time of day. Treat them like you would someone who rings your doorbell at 2:00 a.m. Regardless of their sweet words, you're not in the mood to negotiate whether to let them in or not. Keep the door locked and take up the matter with your new landlord. Remember the scriptural advice, "Keep your heart with all vigilance, for from it flow the springs of life" (Proverbs 4:23).

Sinful thoughts may reappear under a different label— as friends rather than enemies. They will remind you that other Christians struggle with lust too—"it's part of being human." They also may encourage you to pity yourself—"you deserve a break today."

By now those thoughts aren't knocking on the door, they're pulling it off the hinges. Related thoughts gather to reinforce them and you realize you're about to be overwhelmed.

What shall you do?

Thank God for the temptation and view it as an opportunity to prove that Christ is stronger than the flesh. Recall that the Holy Spirit drove Christ into the wilderness to be tempted of the devil. God has allowed you to be brought to this moment because He's teaching you some lessons you couldn't learn otherwise.

Remind yourself that you are in Christ, seated above every principality and power. Because of what He has done, you need not submit to this temptation. Anchor your soul in the assurance that these enemies have already been conquered.

Remember that your real struggle is not with the temptation but with God. Whether you say *yes* or *no*, He is the one to whom you are answerable. To some degree you're accountable to yourself and to others, but ultimately, you report to God. The real question is: Will you believe Him? Will you honor Him or grieve Him?

Quote verses of Scripture which assure you of victory.

You are fighting from a position of strength. Once again I want to emphasize that the flesh and Satan tell lies. They want to overwhelm you and make you think you have to obey your passions. In Christ, you don't!

Don't be put off by repeated temptations. Satan will try to wear down your resistance, but continue to submit your mind fully to God.

## LONG-RANGE EFFECTS

"And we all, with unveiled face, beholding the glory of the Lord, are being transformed into the same image from one degree of glory to another. For this comes from the Lord who is the Spirit" (2 Corinthians 3:18). Christlikeness comes when we behold in the Word of God, the glory of the Lord. We are transformed as we meditate on Him as He is seen in the Scriptures.

Remember Nathaniel Hawthorne's story of the great stone face? Some rocks on the side of a mountain had been thrown together in such a way as to resemble the features of a man. When the little boy, Ernest, inquired about the expression on the face, which was both noble and sweet, his mother told him a story that passed on from one generation to another: In some future day, a child would be born who would be the greatest person of his time and he would resemble the great stone face.

Ernest never forgot the story. When a rumor spread

throughout the valley that a man was coming who resembled the stone face, he was as excited as the other people in the valley. But Ernest was disappointed. The man was greedy, and his face didn't have the kindness of the great stone face.

Ernest spent every free moment gazing at the glorious features and yearned for the day when the right man would come to the valley. Other men appeared, but they never resembled the great stone face.

Ernest, at middle age, was thoughtful and generous. Neither his friends nor he, least of all, suspected that he was more than an ordinary man. By the time he was an old man, he was full of wisdom and kindness. People came from far and near to talk with him.

One day a poet who had heard of Ernest came to the valley. Ernest listened to the poet and was so impressed that he thought his new friend bore a resemblance to the beautiful features of the stone face. But the poet said he was unworthy of such an honor.

As Ernest addressed an audience gathered in the open air, the poet recognized that Ernest was the likeness of the great stone face he had gazed at for so long. *We become what we gaze at.*

We will never be Christlike by trying to resist temptation, as necessary as that may be. We must fill our minds with the wonder of Jesus Christ and have an insatiable desire to be like Him. Then slowly, perhaps imperceptibly, we are transformed into the image of Christ. Our temptations, which were so powerful, lose their attraction when we become consumed with all that Christ means to us. Paul said, "That I may know him and the power of his resurrection, and may share his sufferings, becoming like him in his death" (Philippians 3:10).

## STUDY AND APPLICATION

1. The best way to have our minds renewed is to memorize Scripture—daily. Read and reread whole chapters until the words and ideas are fixed firmly in mind—forever. Begin with Psalm 1; John 15:1–11; and Colossians 3:1–11.

2. Using a concordance or an online Bible search tool to find verses of Scripture which relate directly to other battles you may be facing in your life. Memorize these verses as well.

3. Learn to use your temptations as an "alarm system." As soon as certain thoughts enter your mind, reject them, quoting the Scriptures you've learned.

4. Spend 20 minutes with God before 9:00 a.m. every morning. During that time of prayer and Bible reading, claim God's promises for victory that day.

## CHAPTER TWELVE

# RESISTING SATAN'S STRATEGIES

"The nightmares I had become accustomed to over the years subsided; but a much more real harassment began to assert itself. Tinkering with the occult had been deliciously exciting, but when Christ entered the picture, Satan began to show his true colors—colors of fear, confusion, and doubt. The devil becomes angry when he loses a partner in crime. But with Jesus on my side the demon is like a roaring lion without teeth."[48]

Any Christian who is serious about holy living will be in conflict with the devil, or more accurately, with demons who are under the devil's control. People who have given themselves over to sensuality at some point in their lives will probably be overrun by evil thoughts and impulses. Because our sexual desires are so much a part of us, and because sexual purity is necessary for successful family living, we can expect that Satan will make sex a battleground. He will assure us that pleasure and companionship are available outside of God's prescribed will, and that the consequences can be hidden.

Satan strikes, overwhelms, controls, and since he has no moral scruples, he uses every imaginable form of deceit in his arsenal. Every believer is his sworn enemy. He promises freedom, but always enslaves; he tantalizes with pleasure, but always demeans.

- A woman whose mind is filled with sensuality says she cannot sing hymns in church without giving the words a double (sexual) meaning, or read words from the Bible without sexual innuendos. Everything she sees is polluted.

- A father becomes sexually stimulated by his daughter who is scarcely two years old. He can't trust himself to be alone with her.

- A teenage girl had such compulsive sexual desires that she propositioned any man who approached her. When the police came to pick her up, she urged them to have sex with her.

- A Christian college student was arrested for public indecencies. He would expose himself as he walked down the street.

- A man desired (and had) sexual intercourse with animals. He could only think of sex between human beings in perverted and bizarre ways.

Many live with fantasies and passions they share with

no one else for fear of rejection. They believe they are weird, different, and of no worth to God or others. One common misconception is believing they have committed "the unpardonable sin." They are convinced God cannot tolerate them anymore. They hate themselves and believe that if God is righteous, He must surely hate them too. They live within the walls of their own prisons of fear, anxiety, and belief that they are beyond hope. They've tried to make promises to themselves and God, only to repeat their behavior.

They desperately need to share their inner conflicts with someone who will accept them, but not their behavior. This is why fellowship in church is most important. As one writer put it, "What you need is to warm your soul in the sunshine of another person's respect and understanding, and in so doing begin to rediscover respect for yourself."[49]

We derive our understanding of who we are from our parents and other people. If a vice lies hidden within us, and we fear telling someone, we will bear those burdens in the torment of loneliness. Sharing the need is necessary, but usually it's only a beginning. When we have given ourselves to persistent sin, we are engaged in spiritual warfare; Satan needs direct confrontation. We must learn to resist him and weaken his grasp on us.

Satan's intense interest in us is not because he thinks we have intrinsic value. He would like to destroy us and would do so instantly if God didn't prevent him. He wants to ruin us as a way to get back at God. He hates us with the same passion he hates Christ. If we succumb to sin, saying, "That's just the way I am," Satan gloats.

## LOOKING AT HIS STRATEGY

Here are some common methods Satan uses to beguile us and lead us into sin.

*Satan works undercover.* He and the wicked spirits he controls stay in the background so they are not easily detected. Like plainclothes detectives, they prefer to work unrecognized. Satan's goal is to have us serve him while we think we are serving ourselves. His suggestions are passed onto us so deftly we think they're our own.

His first "cover" is the flesh. "Now the works of the flesh are evident: sexual immorality, impurity, sensuality, idolatry, sorcery, enmity, strife, jealousy, fits of anger, rivalries, dissensions, divisions, envy, drunkenness, orgies, and things like these" (Galatians 5:19–21). When we struggle with sensuality, we generally attribute it to the flesh, but demons use the flesh to intensify our desires. That's why it's not always possible to distinguish between the works of the flesh and the works of Satan—they blend into one.

Demons watch us and then concentrate on our most vulnerable weakness. They wear one of a dozen different masks corresponding to the works of the flesh. They'll take fleshly desire and pervert it, inflame it, and make us think we were "born that way." Along with magnified desires comes guilt, and the mind is preoccupied with a sense of helplessness. A good word for this is *obsession*. Satan doesn't care whether it's pornography, adultery, greed, or other forms of sinful thoughts and behavior. As long as the Holy Spirit is grieved, and joy has drained from our lives, Satan is appears to be winning.

A second form of disguise is the human mind.

In a previous chapter, I referred to Ananias and Sapphira who lied about the amount of money they received for a piece of property. Covetousness kept them from being straightforward. They saw a perfect opportunity to be honored in the church and, at the same time, to keep a nest egg for a rainy day. Why not tell a white lie? They didn't have to sell any of the property, as Peter so clearly told them (Acts 5:4), but they wanted to be honored, and after a thoughtful discussion, agreed to lie.

Peter asked, "Ananias, why has Satan filled your heart to lie to the Holy Spirit?" (Acts 5:3). They were not aware that Satan was personally present in their home; they never dreamed he had planted the suggestion in their minds, hoping they'd pick up on it. As far as they were concerned, it was nothing more than their decision.

The New Testament teaches that Satan is involved in

situations such as a fear of witnessing for Christ (Luke 22:31–32); adultery (1 Corinthians 7:5); holding a grudge (2 Corinthians 2:10–11); and evil betrayals (John 13:27). In these and a hundred different situations, Satan and his hosts are actively planting lies in the human mind.

"So then the devil made me do it!" you say. Not quite. He gave you the idea, but you chose to run with it, and because you chose to, God holds you responsible. Adam and Eve tried to blame one another, and even blame Satan. It was he who tempted Eve to eat. What does God say? He says each must bear the consequences of rebellion (see Genesis 3:14–21).

Satan's strategy is to inflame the desires of the body and plant rationalizations in the mind. Because of these disguises, we often are completely unaware that we've been duped. We're like the soldier who sits in his barracks, refusing to believe the reality of war even while his building is being shelled.

*Satan causes spiritual blindness during temptation.* Satan not only injects ideas into our minds, but causes us to be blind to sin's consequences. At the moment of temptation, we can forget verses of Scripture; we won't remember the guilt, anxiety, and tears that follow sexual sin. Christ said Satan snatches the seed of the Word of God from the human mind (Mark 4:15). Peter did not remember Christ's prediction that he'd deny Christ until after the rooster crowed.

Temptations can come to us and put us into a euphoric trance. A man who met an unusually enticing woman in a bus depot was so carried away by her charms that he found himself asking her to meet him in a motel room. "I didn't even know what I was saying...I couldn't have cared who was watching or whether we'd get caught—only one thing mattered."

In Proverbs, there is an apt description of such an experience. The one who is seduced by a harlot follows her "as an ox goes to the slaughter...till an arrow pierces its liver; as a bird rushes into a snare; he does not know that it will cost him his life" (Proverbs 7:22–23). An animal cannot think beyond its perceptions. It thinks neither about God nor tomorrow. Only its immediate desires matter. When spiritual truths are pushed out of our minds, we act like animals. "I don't know why I did it. It's just not like me—it was so stupid!"

No one was ever lured into alcoholism by seeing a drunk staggering along a street covered with his own vomit. Nor is one led into adultery by seeing broken homes and weeping children. Such consequences are often out of view. As Christ said to the Jews who had rejected their Messiah, "[These things] are hidden from your eyes" (Luke 19:42).

*Satan skillfully uses the art of the slow approach.* Often Satan strikes suddenly, but he uses the slow approach with those who are committed Christians. He moves us from the familiar to the unfamiliar. He gives us time to rationalize, to make excuses as to why we want to see a particular person or be in a certain place where we know we will be tempted. He is gratified when we sin in our minds and it appears to have no harmful effects—he likes us to believe we can handle our own sins when we really become serious about them. He's not concerned about whether our sin is big or little; he's concerned about our perception of sin itself. The little sins will eventually become big as long as we think we are able to contain them.

A con artist in the city of Chicago persuaded a businessman to give him $5,000 for an investment. At the end of three months, the man returned $10,000 to the investor. He repeated the same tactic, always careful to give the investor a high rate of return. Trust was developed between them. One day the con man asked for $50,000 and got it. That was the last time they met.

Remember Samson? His weakness was women, particularly the women of the Philistines. He said *no* to Delilah three times before he gave in and told her the source of his strength. Mark it well: Satan doesn't care how many times we say *no* to temptation as long as we stay in the vicinity of it because eventually, he'll get us.

Time is on his side. Give him an inch today and he's prepared to wait five years before he gets his mile. The process of sin is never static, it must move backward or forward because no compromise is possible. Even if the pendulum moves back and forth, Satan is satisfied. Someday when we're dozing, we will fall into his well-planned trap.

What shall we learn from the slow approach? Even if we are victorious today, we can't be sure of future victories. The sense of self-confidence and well-being we have today can drive us down the path of destruction tomorrow. The victories of the past are no guarantee of victory in the future.

*Satan works through guilt.* He tries to get us to feel so defeated that we give up the idea of moral resistance. He prefers that we either feel no guilt whatsoever or be burdened with excessive guilt. Most Christians want to feel guilty when they fall into sin. After all, they want to prove their moral sensitivity to themselves, and guilt is a testimony of their relationship with God. Some people, however, feel guilty for not feeling guilty. Like one man put it, "I expected God to rain judgment from heaven when I walked into that strip club. Yet I went to work the next day as usual, the sky didn't fall in. It's been a few weeks now, and I've still not confessed my sin because I don't feel as bad about what I did as I thought I would. I suspect I'll do it again."

Paul talks about seductive spirits who lure people away from the truth; "seared in their own conscience as with a branding iron" (1 Timothy 4:2, NASB). The *Chicago*

*Tribune* carried a story of a man jailed for committing more than twenty rapes. Despite the terror he caused these women (one of them attempted suicide later), he said he had no guilt until after he was arrested. He did it without a twinge of conscience.

The opposite side of the coin is excessive guilt. Some people are convinced they're too terrible for God to forgive. They're running away from God, thinking He would prefer to see them dead. Unfortunately, they consider themselves to be unworthy of God's grace. So as long as they hate themselves, Satan has won a victory. If you feel overburdened with guilt, he will get you to believe you are beyond forgiveness. If you don't feel as guilty as you should, he will get you to believe you lack appropriate sorrow for your sin. Either way, you will be kept from God's grace.

*He inflames resentment against God.* Back in the Garden of Eden, Satan accused God of being evil. He implied that God didn't desire the best for Adam and Eve. Satan uses the same strategy today. Many people (including Christians) rise up in rebellion against God, arguing that God is unfair in restricting them. God, they believe, is repressive and does not have their good in mind. A woman who enjoys sexual fulfillment lives with a husband who is impotent. Isn't it only right that she find a man who can appreciate her physical beauty and give her the satisfaction she craves? Or what about the single person, caught in a web of loneliness and seeking the intimacy that would meet the desires planted within every human being? Resentment against God lies at the heart of many of our rationalizations.

The cause of Satan's downfall was rebellion, and some of that poison has fallen onto every human heart. When we become angry with God, we are taking sides with Satan. He delights that we are agreeing with him.

## THE WAY TO FREEDOM

*Recognize Christ's Authority.* Unfortunately, the ascension of Christ is often thought of as an article of the creeds. But in the New Testament, the ascension is presented as positive proof that Jesus has conquered every enemy. In Ephesians we read of Jesus, "That he [God] worked in Christ when he raised him from the dead and seated him at his right hand in the heavenly places, far above all rule and authority and power and dominion, and above every name that is named, not only in this age but also in the one to come. And he put all things under his feet and gave him as head over all things to the church" (Ephesians 1:20–22).

Christ is seated at the right hand of God. The Old Testament priests stood at the brazen altar offering sacrifices. They never had a chance to sit down because their work was never completed. But Christ sits; the victory has been won. Also, Jesus is not merely above all principalities and powers but *far* above them. The symbolism is obvious: His victory wasn't even close; the outcome was never in doubt. He won decisively and with finality. His foes are now His footstool. The nations may rage and take counsel against the Lord but "He who sits in the heavens laughs; the Lord holds them in derision" (Psalm 2:4). Satan can rant and rave; he can threaten and demean; he can seduce and deceive, but his humiliation is already history. In a matter of time, he will be exposed for what he is and be thrown into the lake of fire forever (Revelation 20:10).

Christ's position at the right hand of God the Father denotes high honor. He has ready access to the Father and is assured of unqualified acceptance. Jesus crushed the head of the serpent and the devil knows it.

How can we reconcile the fact that believers are in Christ and share His victory with the fact that Satan makes such deep inroads into their lives?

First, we must apply Christ's victory by faith; that is, regardless of our temptations, there must be a firm insistence that Christ has indeed triumphed. Even then, victory isn't automatic. Jesus gave the disciples authority over all demons, yet later the disciples confronted a demon that wouldn't respond to them. Jesus rebuked them for their lack of faith and added that some do not come out except by prayer and fasting (Matthew 17:21). God wants to teach us that faith must be built up in our hearts, and triumph can never be thoughtlessly assumed.

God lets us struggle with Satan to teach us about the nature of sin and our own weakness. If our successes were always instantaneous, we'd begin to think, *Sin isn't so bad after all. I can enjoy it and be forgiven whenever I like and get out of it without a hassle.* Spiritual conflict is a means of God's discipline to let us know how destructive sin can be.

If an Israeli soldier wanders into a Palestinian army camp (or vice versa), he's in for a long struggle. He may plead it happened in ignorance or without harmful intent. No matter. He can appeal on the basis of his citizenship, but he's not going to be returned without the scars of battle. He'll have learned a powerful lesson about where the boundaries are and where he ought to take his "vacation" next year.

Those who are victimized by compulsive sensuality usually know where they have crossed the line, whether through incest, pornography, or extramarital sex. Sometimes they've walked deliberately into Satan's territory, the world which lies in his power (1 John 5:19). They want to be free, but they are struggling.

The first step is to know that Satan's defeat is already accomplished. Visualize Christ seated at the right hand of God with His enemies beneath Him. Then see yourself with Christ.

*Renounce Sin.* Sometimes we underestimate the intensity of the conflict with our passions. We think victory comes by simply knowing who we are in Christ and then confidently facing whatever comes along. But our enemy tries to use our past as a launching pad for his attacks against us.

The admonition, "Give no opportunity to the devil" (Ephesians 4:27), could be translated, "Don't give the devil a place of dwelling." We are not to give him any reason for thinking he can continue to control us.

When people enter another country illegally, it's often difficult to have them deported, especially if they've lived there illegally for a number of years. They insist they've earned the right to continue to live there. We must resist Satan and renounce those practices that have put us on his turf. Here are some sins that must be renounced in the name of Jesus Christ.

- Occult practices, such as fortune telling, the Ouija board, astrology, palmistry, ESP, and reading horoscopes. Ask God to bring to mind those involvements that may give Satan license to harass you.

- Sensual practices, such as alcohol, drugs, illicit sex, mind control, and pornography.

- The influence of others over you. The second commandment says God allows the effects of idol worshipers to continue in a family until the third and fourth generations (see Exodus 20:5–6). Those who are in cults often have fallen into idolatry.

Renounce any influence which may have come via your ancestors or even those who have been trying to help you while they themselves are under satanic control.

Sometimes God instantly delivers a person from compulsive behavior and thoughts. At other times, it's a slow, steady process. Though God gave the Israelites the whole land, He told Joshua that the enemies would be driven out "little by little" (Deuteronomy 7:22).

The question is whether we are willing to completely repent of all sin and willingly submit to whatever discipline may come as a result of disobedience. If we know who we are in Christ, we have a *right* to be free from moral slavery.

*Keep Up The Conflict.* A believer will often resist Satan with great success and think, "At last, I'm free!" That's a dangerous moment. A sense of self-confidence, even when it appears to be God-directed, can set us up for another fall. When that happens, Satan will make us think victory isn't worth the price. He'll make sure we remember the pleasure of sensuality without being able to recall the sorrow that accompanied it. When we find ourselves back at square one, we think, *There's nothing to it after all...just as I suspected!*

But if Satan attacks us a hundred times, we are to resist a hundred times. Christ was harassed three times in rapid succession. Resisting Satan is not something we do twice a week; it's whenever we find our minds being drawn away to former lusts. We must develop sensitivity to the first promptings of the Holy Spirit. When the enemy overwhelms us, we must say, "I reject this thought in Jesus' name."

That doesn't mean the battle is over. Desire may even intensify. Satan's goal is to throw us off balance by creating unbelief in our hearts. He'll suggest a hundred different reasons why the Scriptures don't really work; he'll get us to think we are different.

What are we to do? Submit ourselves to God and stand our ground. Insist we belong to Christ, and that Satan has no authority over us. Pray a prayer of resistance.

*Put On The Armor Of God.* If we are fighting a lion, we don't do it with bare hands. If we are up against tanks, a slingshot won't do. God lists the pieces of spiritual armor needed to stand against the wiles of the devil. I'm glad He doesn't expect us to gain new territory, but simply stand on the ground that Jesus already conquered (Ephesians 6:10–20).

We can't cover the pieces of armor in detail, but notice they include honesty, righteousness, witnessing, faith, correct thinking, and the use of prayer and intercession. If any piece is missing, that's where we can expect an attack.

Remember this battle is against spirits who are wicked, unprincipled, and destructive. They are, by nature, liars. If they tell the truth, it's only to deceive. They are mean, vicious, and bold. Don't expect them to give pleasure in sin without returning to collect.

Paul uses the expression, "in the heavenlies" five times in the book of Ephesians. He uses the same expression in connection with our struggle, indicating that when we really become serious about our relationship with God, we're in for spiritual conflict.

We must pray individually and collectively that we will stand against Satan and say like Paul who, when dealing with carnality in the Corinthian church, urged them to deal with sin, "so that we would not be outwitted by Satan; for we are not ignorant of his designs" (2 Corinthians 2:11). Ignorance about Satan and his ways leads to division, anger, and multiplied sins of every sort.

*Have A Ready Response To Satan.* We have to tie all this information together so it can be used at a moment's notice. We may not have a half-hour's warning, for Satan can strike in seconds. I like what the Puritan writer Gibbon wrote about being prepared for the conflict. I think you might like to put these words in a prominent place where you can remind yourself of them regularly:

"Provide thyself with answers and retorts beforehand, against the subtle insinuations and delusions of thine enemy. For example: If Satan tells thee, as he often will, that the sin is pleasant, ask whether the gripings of conscience be so too, whether it be such a pleasant thing to be in hell, to be under the wrath of an Almighty Judge! If he tells thee, 'Nobody sees; thou mayest commit it safely;' ask whether he can put out God's all-seeing eye, whether he can find a place empty of the Divine presence for thee to sin in, or whether he can blot out the items out of the book of God's remembrance...If he talks of profits and earthly advantages that will accrue, ask what account it will turn to at the last day, and what profit there is if one should gain the whole world and lose his own soul, or what one should give in exchange for his soul! When sin, like Jael, invites thee into her tent, with the lure and decoy of a lordly treatment, think of the nail and hammer which fastened Sisera dead to the ground."[50]

Paul warned, "But I am afraid that as the serpent deceived Eve by his cunning, your thoughts will be led astray from a sincere and pure devotion to Christ" (2 Corinthians 11:3). We cannot let Satan have an advantage over us just because we are ignorant of his devices.

*See A Counselor.* In some cases it's necessary to go to a pastor or Christian worker who has experience in dealing with demonic warfare or addictive behavior. Though Satan cannot possess Christians (possession implies an ownership that belongs to God alone), he can invade a life, particularly if we have opened the door to evil influences. The New Testament speaks of a person being "demonized," a specific harassment, and even a demon (or demons) indwelling of the human body. People who have given themselves over to Satan before they became Christians, or who have been in the occult, may need to confront wicked spirits directly. Although there is controversy about the extent that demons can harass believers, I believe there have been times when believers have had to confront demons and have them expelled.

Satan's greatest weapon at this point is fear. He'll make you think you are better off in your bondage than to go through the hassle of direct conflict. Don't believe it. He's afraid his influence is soon to be over. He wants us to forget who we are in Christ and settle for a life of failure. That's not the will of God, and it isn't necessary. The book, *The Adversary*, by Mark Bubeck (Moody Publishers, 2013) has been of great help to many who need specific instruction on demonic deliverance.

As someone once said to me: "I couldn't shake myself free of immorality. I begged God to change me; I knew all the theology of victory, but it wouldn't work for me. No way. One day it came to a head. I was resisting a particular temptation for a half hour, but was overwhelmed by it. I was angry knowing I would give in again. I called a Christian brother and shared honestly what was happening. Together we rebuked Satan, and after a time, a great sense of peace came to me. It was so great to be free! That doesn't mean I'm not tempted anymore, but I know victory is possible."

Can you identify?

## STUDY AND APPLICATION

1. Memorize verses of Scripture to claim instantly when you're in spiritual warfare (1 John 4:4; James 4:6–7; 1 Peter 5:8–9; Ephesians 2:6).

2. After your past has been cleansed, learn to obey the first promptings of the Holy Spirit. The easiest time to resist temptation is the moment it comes to mind—it will never get easier. If necessary say, "Be gone Satan for it is written," then quote verses of Scripture you have memorized.

3. Ask God to show you any excuses you've used to indulge your mind or body in sensuality. Be sure you have repented of these rationalizations.

4. Spend at least five minutes quoting Scripture before you fall asleep. This will cleanse your mind and guard it from wayward thoughts that often appear early in the morning.

5. Ponder Christ's words, "Sin no more, that nothing worse may happen to you" (John 5:14). What does this tell us about God's discipline for sinning flippantly?

6. Study the pieces of armor listed in Ephesians 6:10–

20. What pieces do we tend to overlook? What can we do to wear this armor more consistently?

7. Learn to pray in warfare against Satan. For example, "Heavenly Father, I bow in worship and praise before you. I surrender myself completely and unreservedly to you. I take a stand against all the workings of Satan that would hinder me in this time of prayer, and I address myself to the only true and living God and refuse any involvement of Satan in my prayer." Then praise God the Father, and affirm your position in Jesus Christ and put on the armor of God.

ERWIN W. LUTZER

CHAPTER THIRTEEN
# EMOTIONAL HEALING

Sexual obsessions are destroying the emotional stability of our young people, our families, and society in general. One half of all divorces happen because one partner falls in love with someone more appealing to them. Given the frightening number of divorces, just over one half of all children born this year will be reared by a single parent at some point.[51] Add to that over 40 percent of births in the US alone are outside of wedlock per year,[52] and we can understand why millions of children are growing up feeling unwanted and emotionally rejected. Decades ago in Viet Nam, American servicemen fathered about 12,000 children who were considered outcasts because of their mixed blood. Many of them starved to death, others lived in the streets and were treated like animals. Many children born in this country feel deep rejection—like the fifteen-year-old girl who was disowned by her parents. They gave away her clothes and sold her bicycle. They didn't want to hear from her again.

Abortion, which is a "mopping-up operation" following in the wake of the sexual revolution, attests to the fact that children are considered disposable, at the whim of the parents.

There are other hurts as well.

Women and girls who have been sexually groomed and even coaxed into bed by demanding boyfriends become resentful in marriage. Guilt and hostility cause frigidity and block the lines of communication. Impotency in men is usually traceable to promiscuity. Tens of thousands are angry because they've contracted a form of STD/STI from some partner they've trusted. They feel betrayed, vindictive.

The need for emotional healing multiplies each year as sexual immorality leaves its scars on the human psyche. When a child is unsure about whether they are wanted; or when a woman sees her husband transfer his affections to someone else, the human spirit is crushed. In fact, emotional pain is more difficult to accept than a physical disease. "A man's spirit will endure sickness, but a crushed spirit who can bear?" (Proverbs 18:14).

Consider this story: A married woman in a moment of unguarded passion had a sexual relationship with her husband's brother. Soon after, she became pregnant, and for 20 years lived with the haunting knowledge that her husband was not be the biological father of their daughter.

When her husband was in a car accident, the whole family pulled together, hoping for his recovery. Months later, he died, not knowing his wife's secret. After the funeral, the mother could bear the guilt no longer. She told her daughter the whole story.

You can guess the effect this had on her daughter when she learned that her uncle was, in fact, her father. She spiraled out of control—drugs, drink, illicit sex, and every form of perversion. And now that the secret was out, her uncle found himself divorced from his wife.

What caused this plunge into moral ruin? The daughter's security and sense of self-worth was snatched from her in a single confession from her mother's lips. Her mother was now despised in her eyes. The daughter's own origin was shrouded in uncertainty; she was bitter and didn't know who she really was.

Or consider the woman who gave birth to her father's child. One day her son found the family records and when he learned that his grandfather was his father, he committed suicide.

These stories represent tens of thousands who are hostile toward their parents and toward God who seems distant and uninterested in their plight. Their need to be loved and wanted is so great that when it's in doubt, a child or even an adult, cannot cope.

Some people seek self-worth by pursuing promising

sexual relationships. For example, a girl who doesn't have a strong loving father will crave the affection of a man who professes to love her. She'll sacrifice her virginity if that's the price she must pay to establish self-esteem and a sense of belonging. When the relationship turns sour (as it must), her self-esteem is further destroyed, after which, she's even worse off. Thus the cycle of insecurity is repeated. The next step may be drugs or alcohol. Many simply cannot handle the raw pain of rejection.

In a report on teenage alcoholism in Chicago, the bottom line was that the young people of today are so insecure because of the breakup of the home, that they cannot tolerate the emptiness they feel. They turn to alcohol and drugs to deaden the emotional pain.

Given the hard facts of illegitimacy, incest, child abuse, and parental failure, can a person be put back together emotionally? Can one's identity and self-worth be firmly established independently of the nuclear family? Is there hope beyond the messes of human relationships?

Here are some starting points toward emotional wholeness.

## FORGIVE THOSE WHO HAVE WRONGED US

It's difficult, but it's possible. Though every fiber of your body revolts against forgiving your parents, spouse, or significant other, it must be done. Bitterness will never change the past; it will not bring the adversary to his knees in humble confession. Chances are the person who has wronged you couldn't care less about how you're feeling. Sin dulls the senses, it deadens the most elementary spark of human decency and kindness.

A person who has sinned sexually and then tried to take care of that blotch on their own (without casting themselves upon the mercy of God) is capable of every form of verbal and physical cruelty. We read of those who are ignorant and have "become callous and have given themselves up to sensuality, greedy to practice every kind of impurity" (Ephesians 4:19). Again, Paul speaks of those who are "seared in their own conscience as with a branding iron" (1 Timothy 4:2, NASB).

This explains why a father who leaves his family can ignore the feelings of his children. They may cry out to him for recognition and acceptance, but he won't even send them a birthday card. I've known children to weep, hoping their fathers will love them, but such fathers are too selfish to see beyond their own physical needs. In a word, a person who gives themselves to sensuality is dehumanized. Only what they see, think, and feel matters; the feelings of others are irrelevant.

Such people seldom admit their failures and ask for forgiveness. God alone can bring them to their senses. Apart from a miracle, their hearts of stone will never be exchanged for hearts of flesh (Ezekiel 11:19).

So, we must forgive those who have wronged us even if they never ask for forgiveness; chances are they won't. In such cases, forgiveness is primarily an act done for our own good. Hostility will ruin any chance for emotional wholeness. We must forgive even when there is no hope of reconciliation.

But how can we forgive? By reminding ourselves how much God has forgiven us. That's the standard of the New Testament, "Forgiving one another, as God in Christ forgave you" (Ephesians 4:32). Forgive whether we feel like it or not. It's a choice we make regardless of how painful it becomes.

And if the bitterness lingers? Forgiving is both an act and a process. We can forgive and perhaps the bitterness may return, but we must reject it in Christ's name. In faith, affirm our trust in the promises of God. We might want to even the score, but that's God's responsibility. "Beloved, never avenge yourselves, but leave it to the wrath of God, for it is written, 'Vengeance is mine, I will repay, says the Lord'" (Romans 12:19).

A woman hid her affair from her husband for two years. Through repentance, she successfully dealt with feelings of guilt and shame, but she felt that one more step had to be taken. She had to confess to her husband what had happened. He reacted angrily and was emotionally devastated. He couldn't believe such a thing could happen to a couple that had been happily married for ten years. For a long time, he refused to forgive; there was little verbal communication, and no sexual intimacy.

It would be easy to say the wife made a mistake in sharing this secret with him. But she could not live with a lie; her mistake was that she should have confessed this to her husband in the presence of a pastor or counselor. Thankfully, in this case, their relationship was restored over time. There are so many of these instances in which it is wise to discuss the situation and next steps with a wise, trusted counselor.

The prophet Hosea, at God's instruction, married a woman named Gomer. She was an adulteress, and even had a child by one of her lovers, hence his name, Lo-Ammi (meaning "not my people"). Then she became a prostitute, flitting from one man to another. Yet the prophet waited for her return and even bought her at a slave auction when her life of sin had run its course. The prediction for Gomer was now one of hope, "And I will betroth you to me forever. I will betroth you to me in righteousness and in justice, in steadfast love and in mercy. I will betroth you to me in faithfulness. And you shall know the LORD" (Hosea 2:19–20).

Clearly, she was fully restored and even regarded as a pure woman again. In fact, "she shall sing there, as in the days of her youth" (Hosea 2:15, KJV). Of course we should not conclude that adultery can simply be forgiven and the marriage continue; issues of repentance, trust, and affection need to be addressed. But there are some times when the bird with a broken wing soars once again.

Jesus reserves harsh judgment for those who refuse to be as gracious in their forgiveness as God is in His. The forgiven servant who would not forgive his fellow servant was handed over to the torturers until he should repay all that was owed by him. Then Christ adds, "So also my heavenly Father will do to every one of you, if you do not forgive your brother from your heart" (Matthew 18:35). Often when there has been betrayal in marriage, given time and following biblical counsel, the relationship can be restored.

Deborah Roberts, a Christian girl who was raped while doing visitation for a church on Chicago's south side, learned that wholeness comes by feeling worthy and valuable again. She lost her virginity and with it, her self-respect. How could she forgive the rapist? She knew the feelings of guilt and shame would never leave her unless she was prepared to forgive. After months of hurt, she concluded, "No one should ever be given the privilege of robbing someone else of their sense of dignity. What I mean is this: If you live perpetually with a sense of guilt and shame because of someone else's sin, you are really letting them control you.

What a tragedy if Roger Gray had permanent control over the life of Deborah Roberts and she would not have been able to rebuild herself."[53]

Do you really want your parents, wife, or husband to control you? Do you really want them to dictate how you will feel and determine the degree of your bitterness? Are they the ones who determine your self-worth? You must choose to forgive if, for no other reason, you deserve it yourself. In Christ's name, choose to forgive.

God has a special family, His family is for people just like you. And He is the Father of all who believe. Our Father in heaven can make up for the failures of our earthly father.

## FORGIVE GOD

Forgiving people is one thing, but what about God? Is He not the sovereign Lord of the universe? Job railed against God because he didn't die in the womb; that would have been better than the tragedies that he was expected to accept.

God could have banished Satan to another planet, or created a man who would choose to obey Him. "Where was He when my father and brother raped me at the age of ten?" a young woman in her 20s asked with bitterness. "What kind of a God is He if He watched without doing anything?"

That's exactly the same question Deborah Roberts faced. After reading Psalm 121 with its great promises of God's keeping power and guidance in the life of a Christian, Deborah asked, "What about that, God? Shouldn't I believe Your promises? I thought I was special to You. Did I read that wrong or wasn't that a promise from You to protect me? I just don't understand. Are You a loving God or are you a vengeful God? Do You have a reason for me to be raped? Did you really want that to happen to me? What reason could be good enough for that kind of pain? I nearly killed myself over it. Do You remember that?"[54]

Her ultimate conclusion is the one we are forced to accept: God's love does not prevent us from the tragedies of sexual abuse or any other kind of mistreatment. Christ was God's "beloved Son," yet the Father didn't shield Him from the torture of crucifixion. That crime, despite its horror, has become for us a fountain of blessing. The horror of Good Friday must be understood in the light of the joy of Easter Sunday.

God can do the same with the ugly hurts of life. Jephthah was an illegitimate child, yet God used him mightily (Judges 11:1, 29, 32). Rahab was a prostitute, but became a special heroine of faith (Hebrews 11:31).

When you become angry with God, you're actually trading places with Him. You are trying to become greater than God by bringing Him into your law court and putting

Him on trial. Alexander Pope spoke of those who wished to indict God. They:

> Snatch from his hand the balance and the rod,
> Rejudge his justice, be the God of God.[55]

Confess the bitterness you have toward Him. Concentrate on His infinite grace and be forgiven and accepted. Someone has said that God can put anyone back together as long as we give Him all the pieces. Don't minimize the injustice and sin done against you. But admit your need for God. Bitterness must be surrendered.

## SEE YOURSELF AS VALUABLE TO GOD

Self-hatred is one of the devil's most effective weapons. When we reject ourselves, we are demeaning the highest order of God's earthly creation.

Those who have been mistreated often blame themselves for their lot in life, even though they may be the victims of other people's sins. Children of divorced parents may think they were the cause of the split; a child forced into an incestuous relationship feels dirty; and a girl raped by a sexual maniac is overcome by self-contempt. False guilt is just as devastating as real guilt if not resolved.

God wants us to feel good about ourselves. That is, we must thank Him that we were created by Him, and must be satisfied with the way we look. What is more, we must accept our circumstances as a part of a plan out of which God wants to display His mercy and lovingkindness. Some of the most effective Christian servants I have known were born outside of wedlock; some were unwanted, rejected, but welcomed and used mightily by God, their Father in heaven.

Read the book of Ephesians and jot down all the descriptive terms that apply to us as God's people. We were chosen in Christ before the foundation of the world, adopted, accepted, redeemed from sin's power, and have received the gift of the Holy Spirit. We have become heirs of God and joint heirs with Christ. If the value of an object is dependent on the price paid for it, we rate highly, for we were purchased at high cost (1 Peter 1:18–19). Consequently, our body now belongs to God (1 Corinthians 6:19–20).

Even our physical characteristics are God ordained. David wrote that God meticulously plans the features of the unborn (Psalm 139:13–16). Remember that before we were born, God called us by name and conferred on us the special privilege of being one of His children.

Emotional healing takes time, but the pace is quickened when we accept forgiveness and cleansing. Then we affirm with the Scriptures that we are number one on God's list of priorities in the universe.

## SHARE YOUR STRUGGLES

Have you ever wondered why mere facts sometimes don't work in and of themselves? Those of us who believe in biblical counseling sometimes fall into the trap of thinking the antidote to every problem is information, that the truths of the Scripture must simply be memorized and applied.

Not so.

Relationships are sometimes the key to overcoming personal battles. Just yesterday, a man shared secret struggles he'd never been able to articulate before. When he was finished, I gave him a few suggestions, but they were not nearly as important as the fact that he had been able to share his inner self with another human being. It was a relief for him to be able to share openly and be affirmed and accepted.

We derive the answer to the question "Who am I?" from other people. That's why parents play such a crucial role in helping children establish their identities. But if they fail, the body of Christ has the responsibility of supplying the emotional reinforcements so necessary for healing. We are after all, the continuation of Christ's ministry on Earth. Christ is physically present on Earth through us.

One woman was so filled with self-hatred, she couldn't look at herself in the mirror. She'd just comb her hair out of the corner of her eye, never seeing herself directly. What changed her? Someone told her she was loved and accepted. Then she was hugged and made to feel she was a worthy human being. We'll never know how many emotional problems would be solved if we all exercised the tenderness and concern of Christ our Savior.

## WHO ARE YOU?

A Lutheran minister told seminary students they'd be less likely to fall into moral temptation if they wore their clerical garb. He understood that our perception of ourselves determines how we act.

How do you perceive yourself? If the answer is bitter, angry, guilty, or any other negative adjective, you will steadily slide back into a moral swamp. You will have no reason to look up, no plans to move to higher ground. Your negative thoughts will work themselves into the common habits of everyday life.

Or are you willing to see yourself in a different perspective? Even if you don't feel loved and accepted, are you willing to accept by faith what God says about you? God has painted a portrait of you that is quite different from the one you may have of yourself. He's able to change the way you see yourself, and thereby change your behavior and feelings.

We read of several in the Bible who experienced identity crises. Moses asked God, "Who am I?" God didn't answer his question directly; rather He said, "I AM WHO I AM" (Exodus 3:14). Then God asked him to tell the sons of Israel, "I AM has sent me to you." Moses learned that his self-identity could be understood only with reference to his relationship with God. It really didn't matter who Moses was, as long as Moses knew who God was and was obedient to His will.

Sometimes God actually changed a person's name to give them a new reputation and a new identity. God was communicating His confidence that special blessings lay ahead.

Abram meaning "high father," becomes Abraham "the father of many nations."

Jacob which means "cheater," becomes Israel "a prince of God."

Simon, possibly a derivative of Simeon which means "hearing," is renamed Peter "the rock."

Now it's your turn. What is your name? Is it guilt, anger, sensuality? God wants to give you a new name that identifies you as His special child. To those who overcome He says, "I will give him a white stone, with a new name written on the stone that no one knows except the one who receives it" (Revelation 2:17).

With your past behind you, and your future in God's hands, you can be emotionally whole.

## STUDY AND APPLICATION

1. What kind of childhood experiences erode self-esteem? What responsibilities do parents have in developing self-esteem?

2. How did Christ deal with a woman caught in shame and guilt? (John 8:1–11). What lessons are in this for us?

3. What is the responsibility of the body of Christ toward one another in times of emotional need? Study passages such as Romans 12:5; 14:1–4; 1 Corinthians 12:26–27; Galatians 6:1–5.

4. How did Christ use Peter's failures to develop him? Study passages such as Matthew 14:28–31, 16:16–23, 18:21–22; Luke 5:8–10, 22:31–32; John 6:66–68; 13:1–14, 18:10–11.

5. How does being accepted in Christ provide the foundation for accepting others? (Ephesians 1:6).

CHAPTER FOURTEEN

# FACING TOMORROW

Where do you go from here? Information is of no help unless you are ready to apply it when you need it.

Suppose you lived in a city which was continually under attack. An enemy would harass the inhabitants, leave, and return through the same hole in the wall. Don't you think the citizens should devise a strategy for defense?

Some of us succumb to the same sexual sins again and again, yet we don't take time to "close the hole in the wall." For most of us, our walk with God is a mixed bag. Times of victory are interspersed with times of defeat. The preparations we make during the good times will determine our responses when the temptations come.

Since the mind is the primary battleground, you must guard it carefully by being alert to sinful fantasies and rationalizations.

My soul, be on thy guard;

Ten thousand foes arise;

> The hosts of sin are pressing hard
> To draw thee from the skies.[56]

Do you know precisely what you will do when sensuality comes into your life? Let me encourage you to take time to devise your strategy for that inevitable confrontation.

*Begin by sharing your struggle with one or two people you trust.* You'll be strengthened by their prayerful support, and God will use this act of humility in your life. To admit a need to others is proof that you've come to the end of your own resources. It means you are more concerned about overcoming your sin than you are about what people may think.

## NO SUBSTITUTE FOR SUBMITTING

Repentance begins as an act but must continue as an attitude. We must be willing to accept whatever God brings into our lives. There is no substitute for submitting fully to God before 9:00 a.m. every morning. Don't think that prayer is just talking to God; it's also waiting in quietness, asking Him to show us where we are out of agreement with Him.

Stay current with God on every single issue. Don't let "weeds" (stray thoughts) begin to accumulate, or they will become firmly rooted again. If you've got to pray ten times a day, do it, but stay in fellowship with God, whatever the cost.

## MEDITATE ON THE SCRIPTURES

The Word of God is a cleansing agent. "Already you are clean because of the word that I have spoken to you" (John 15:3). It also fortifies us against sin. "How can a young man keep his way pure? By guarding it according to your word" (Psalm 119:9).

We can unleash the power of God's Word by reading the Scripture every day and writing down in a notebook what we observed in a passage. Nothing can take the place of God's Word occupying our minds. We can memorize verses of Scripture directly related to areas of temptation, and use them at a moment's notice. When temptation comes, we can say, "I resist that temptation in Jesus' name," and quote the verses we've learned.

One man repeated the verse, "Blessed are the pure in heart, for they shall see God" (Matthew 5:8) five times the moment he was confronted with sensual thoughts. *Then* he was able to say *no* to lust and *yes* to God.

## EVERY TEMPTATION IS A STEPPING STONE

You're struggling? We all are, but we have an opportunity to prove Christ is stronger than the flesh. God is using our trials to sift through our lives to separate the temporal from the eternal. He's asking: "Are you willing to give up the cherished pleasures of the heart in favor of fellowship with me?"

Thank God for temptation. We are answerable to Him, and He has allowed testing in our lives because He has lessons to teach us. An attitude of praise for the thorn in the flesh will give God a chance to make His strength perfect in weakness. Memorize psalms of praise to God and concentrate on becoming a worshiper.

*Never give up.* Every failure brings us to a point of fuller surrender to God. We learn that sin is evil and God is righteous. We repent more deeply each time until God brings us to helplessness. The clay totally submits to the Potter.

You should work out the details of your own plan. Know precisely what you will do when temptation comes. Come to the battle prepared—ready for emergencies.

"If you abide in my word, you are truly my disciples, and you will know the truth, and the truth will set you free" (John 8:31–32).

"So if the Son sets you free, you will be free indeed" (v. 36).

# LIVING WITH YOUR PASSIONS

# ENDNOTES

1. Oswald Chambers, *God's Workmanship: And, He Shall Glorify Me* ( Discovery House Publishers, 1997), 35.

2. Bruce Shelley, *Church History in Plain Language, Updated Second Edition* (Nashville: Thomas Nelson, 1996), 126.

3. *Advent Review and Sabbath Herald*, Volume 148, Part 2, (Madison, Wisonsin: Review and Herald Publishing Association, 1971), 16.

4. Augustine, *The Confessions*, X.xxix, https://www.newadvent.org/fathers/110110.htm.

5. Roy Hession, *Forgotten Factors*, (Fort Washington, PA: Christian Literature Crusade, 1980), 60.

6. "Teenage Pregnancy and Teen Abortions—Statistics and Facts," *OpinionFront*, https://opinionfront.com/teenage-pregnancy-teen-abortions-statistics-facts.

7. "Unmarried Childbearing," *Centers for Disease Control and Prevention,* https://www.cdc.gov/nchs/fastats/unmarried-childbearing.htm.

8. CL Shannon and JD Klausner, "The Growing Epidemic of Sexually Transmitted Infections in Adolescents: A Neglected Population," *National Library of Medicine*, PMC 2019 February 1, https://www.ncbi.nlm.nih.gov/pmc/articles/PMC5856484/.

9. Joyce Landorf, *Tough and Tender* (Ada, Michigan: Fleming H. Revell, 1975), 132–133.

10. Warren Wiersbe, *Be Challenged* (Chicago: Moody Press, 1982), 2.

11. "Child Maltreatment Statistics," *American Society for the Positive Care of Children*, AmericanSPCC, https://americanspcc.org/child-maltreatment-statistics/.

12. "The Effects of Sexual Abuse by a Family Member on Survivors and the Importance of Finding a Supportive Community," September 30, 2022, RAINN, https://www.rainn.org/news/effects-sexual-abuse-family-member-survivors-and-importance-finding-supportive-community.

13. Michael Ray Garcia, Stephen W. Leslie, Anton A. Wray, "Sexually Transmitted Infections," *National Library of Medicine,* May 30, 2023, https://www.ncbi.nlm.nih.gov/books/NBK560808/.

14. Péter Apari, João Dinis de Sousa, and Viktor Müller, "Why Sexually Transmitted Infections Tend to Cause Infertility: An Evolutionary Hypothesis," *National Library of Medicine,* August 7, 2014, https://www.ncbi.nlm.nih.gov/pmc/articles/PMC4125283/.

15. Michael Ray Garcia, Stephen W. Leslie, Anton A. Wray, "Sexually Transmitted Infections," *National Library of Medicine,* May 30, 2023, https://www.ncbi.nlm.nih.gov/books/NBK560808/.

16. "10 Things to Know About HIV Suppression," *National Institute of Allergy and Infectious Disease,* June 12, 2020, https://www.niaid.nih.gov/diseases-conditions/10-things-know-about-hiv-suppression.

17. Robert Burns, "Tam O'Shanter," *Poetry Foundation*, https://www.poetryfoundation.org/poems/43815/tam-o-shanter.

18. George Gilder, *Sexual Suicide* (New York: Quadrangle, 1973), 42.

19. Roy Hession, *Forgotten Factors,* (Fort Washington, PA: Christian Literature Crusade, 1980),, 22.

20. C.S. Lewis, *God in the Dock* (Grand Rapids, Michigan: William B. Eerdmans Publishing Company, 2014), 360.

21. C.S. Lewis, *God in the Dock* (Grand Rapids, Michigan: William B. Eerdmans Publishing Company, 2014), 355.

22. Ted Wilhelm Engstrom, editor, *Great Sermons From Master Preachers Of All Ages* (Grand Rapids, MI: Zondervan, 1951), 93.

23. Ted Wilhelm Engstrom, editor, *Great Sermons From Master Preachers Of All Ages* (Grand Rapids, MI: Zondervan, 1951), 107.

24. James Nichols, translator, *Puritan Sermons: 1659-1689: Being the Morning Exercises at Cripplegate, St. Giles in the Fields, and in Southwark, Volume 1*, (Somers, NY: Richard Owen Roberts Publishers, 1981), 53.

25. A.W. Tozer, *The Radical Cross* (Chicago: Moody Publishers, 2015), 47.

26. Christian Nestell Bovee, *Intuitions and Summaries of Thought,*

*Volume 2* (Boston: W. Veazie, 1862), 149.

27. Walter Trobisch, *Love Is A Feeling To Be Learned* (Westmont, IL: InterVarsity Press, 1969), 18.

28. "Autoerotism" in *The Encyclopedia of Sexual Behavior, Volume 1*, A. Ellis and Aborbanel, editors (New York City: Hawthorn Books, 1973), 204.

29. Dr. James Dobson, "A Question About Masturbation," *Dobson Digital Library*, https://dobsonlibrary.com/resource/article/62636b45-ecd9-4346-afde-aa6681775ce2.

30. Walter and Ingrid Trobisch, *My Beautiful Feeling* (Westmont, IL: InterVarsity Press, 1976), 26.

31. Walter and Ingrid Trobisch, *My Beautiful Feeling* (Westmont, IL: InterVarsity Press, 1976), 18.

32. Walter and Ingrid Trobisch, *My Beautiful Feeling* (Westmont, IL: InterVarsity Press, 1976), 116.

33. David W. Augsburger, *Caring Enough To Confront* (Glendale, CA: Regal Books, 1980), 127.

34. Ruth Barnhouse, *Homosexuality: A Symbolic Confusion* (California: Seabury Press, 1977), 139.

35. In chapter 4 of my book, *The Truth about Same-Sex Marriage* (2004, Moody Publishers), I use their research to expand upon common statements by the LGBTQ+ community uses to put pressure on Christians to accept their agenda.

36. Rob Moll, "Civil Unions: Would a Marriage by any Other Name Be the Same?" *Christianity Today,* March 1, 2004, https://www.christianitytoday.com/ct/2004/marchweb-only/3-8-11.0.html.

37. William Justice, *Guilt and Forgiveness* (Baker Book House, 1981), 105.

38. Charles H. Spurgeon, *Treasure of the Bible, Old Testament, Vol. 4* (Grand Rapids, MI: Zondervan), 760.

39. John White, *Daring to Draw Near* (Westmont, IL: InterVarsity Press), 56.

40. Augustine, *The Confessions,* X.xxix, https://www.newadvent.org/fathers/110110.htm.

41. A.W. Tozer, *God's Pursuit of Man* (Chicago: Moody Publishers, 2015), 58.

42. Richard O. Roberts, *Revival* (Wheaton, IL: Richard Owens Roberts Publishing, 1991), 22.

43. John Gibbon, *Puritan Sermons, Volume 1* (Wheaton, IL: Richard Owens Roberts Publishing, 1981), 91.

44. Dr. Howard Taylor and Geraldine Taylor, *Hudson Taylor's Spiritual Secret* (Chicago: Moody Publishers, 2009), 165.

45. Paraphrased from Robert T. Henry, *The Golden Age of Preaching: Men Who Moved the Masses* (Lincoln, NE: iUniverse, 2005), 191.

46. John Bunyon, *Chronicles of Mansoul* (Glendale, CA: Regal Books, 1980), 5.

47. *Leadership Magazine*, Vol. 3 No. 4, 1982, page 43.

48. Terry Bradly, *Moody Monthly*, October 1976, page 130.

49. John White, *Eros Defiled* (Westmont, IL: InterVarsity Press), 144.

50. John Gibbon, *Puritan Sermons, Volume 1* (Wheaton, IL: Richard Owens Roberts Publishing, 1981), 98.

51. Branka Vuleta, "35 Encouraging Stats on the Divorce Rate in America for 2023," *Legaljobs*, May 20, 2023, https://legaljobs.io/blog/divorce-rate-in-america/.

52. "Out of Wedlock Births by Country 2024," *World Population Review*, https://worldpopulationreview.com/country-rankings/out-of-wedlock-births-by-country.

53. Deborah Roberts, *Raped* (Grand Rapids, MI: Zondervan, 1981), 133.

54. Deborah Roberts, *Raped* (Grand Rapids, MI: Zondervan, 1981), 128.

55. Alexander Pope, "An Essay On Man", *Poetry Foundation*, https://www.poetryfoundation.org/poems/44899/an-essay-on-man-epistle-i

56. George Heath "My Soul, Be On Thy Guard," Hymnary.org, https://hymnary.org/text/my_soul_be_on_thy_guard

# LIVING WITH YOUR PASSIONS

Made in the USA
Monee, IL
21 April 2024

57162365R00125